Essays on Architecture

NEW**ARCHITECTURE**

Essays on Architecture

Raimund Abraham · Tadao Ando · Jean Baudrillard · Coop Himmelb(l)au · Peter Eisenman · Dimitri Fatouros · Paul Greenhalgh · Hans Hollein · Arata Isozaki · Toyo Ito · Léon Krier · Kisho Kurokawa · Daniel Libeskind · Marcos Novak · Andreas Papadakis · Ken Powell · Wolf Prix · Patrik Schumacher · Ignasí de Solà Morales · Masaharu Takasaki · Richard Taylor · Bernard Tschumi · Lebbeus Woods

PAPADAKIS PUBLISHER

We gratefully acknowledge the granting of permission to use the images that accompany the essays. Every reasonable attempt has been made to identify and contact the copyright holders. Any errors or omissions are inadvertent and will be corrected in subsequent editions.

Design Director: Alexandra Papadakis
Designer: Magali Nishimura
Editor: Sheila de Vallée

First published in 2007 by Papadakis Publisher
an imprint of New Architecture Group Ltd

11 Shepherd Market, London W1J 7PG
www.papadakis.net

ISBN: 9781901092646

Copyright © 2007 New Architecture Group Ltd
All rights reserved
Individual essays are the copyright of the author

Neither the editors nor New Architecture Group Ltd hold themselves responsible for the opinions expressed by writers of articles in this collection

No part of this publication may be reproduced or transmitted in any form or by any means, electronic or mechanical, including photocopying, recording or any information storage or retrieval system without the written permission of the Publisher

Printed and bound in Singapore

contents

- 8. **Hans Hollein** Sensing the Future: The Architect as Seismograph
- 14. **Raimund Abraham** Jottings
- 20. **Peter Eisenman** Presentness and the "Being-Only-Once" of Architecture
- 34. **Bernard Tschumi** Architecture and Events
- 48. **Kisho Kurokawa** Abstract Geometry and Contemporary Architecture
- 54. **Léon Krier** Prospects for a New Urbanism
- 68. **Coop Himmelb(l)au** The Architecture of Clouds
- 72. **Lebbeus Woods** The Crisis of Innovation
- 84. **Dimitri Fatouros** The End of Place?
- 88. **Daniel Libeskind** Traces of the Unborn
- 94. **Toyo Ito** Three Transparencies
- 104. **Tadao Ando** Beyond Minimalism
- 110. **Masaharu Takasaki** Kagoshima Cosmology
- 116. **Bernard Tschumi** Bodies From Outer Space
- 120. **Ken Powell** Norman Foster's Triumph
- 132. **Jean Baudrillard** Truth and Radicality in Architecture
- 148. **Ignasí de Solà Morales** Present and Futures
- 152. **Wolf Prix** In Between or Only Unstable Points can be Points of Departure
- 162. **Dimitri Fatouros** Philip Johnson's Cathedral of Hope
- 166. **Paul Greenhalgh** The Tensile Line
- 176. **Marcos Novak** Neuro~, Nano~, Bio~: New Atomism and Living Nanotectonics
- 186. **Richard Taylor** Second Nature Fractured Magic from Pollock to Gehry
- 198. **Arata Isozaki** City of Girls Tokyo – An Alien Metropolis
- 204. **Patrik Schumacher** What's Next? From Destructive Impact to Creative Impulse
- 210. **Patrik Schumacher** Aspects of the Work of Zaha Hadid
- 218. **Andreas Papadakis** Philosophy and Architecture, a partnership for the future?

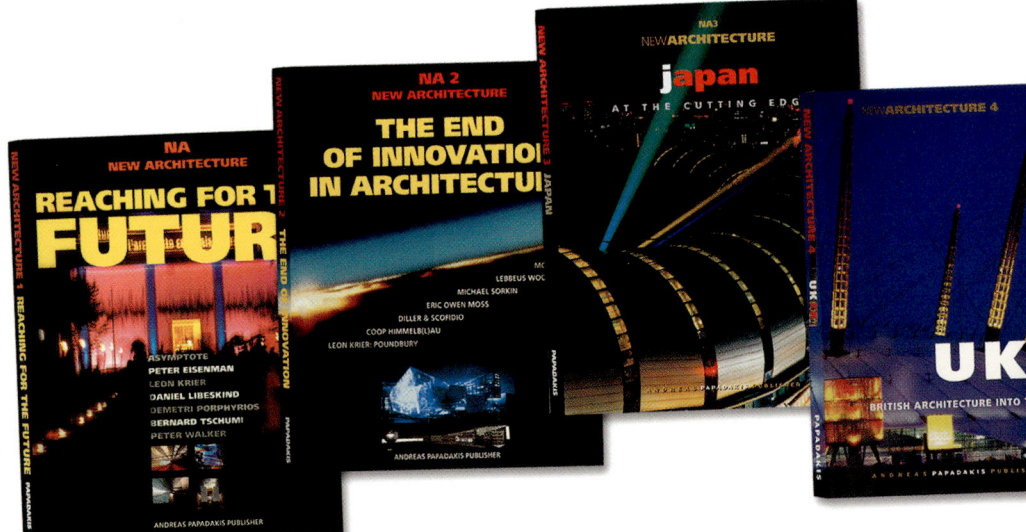

NEW ARCHITECTURE

NA1 Reaching for the Future
NA2 The End of Innovation
NA3 Japan
NA4 UK2K
NA5 Truth, Radicality and Beyond
NA6 Art Nouveau: an Architectural Indulgence
NA7 Innovation
NA8/9 Zaha Hadid

The following extracts and essays are taken from the successive issues of *New Architecture* magazine published over the past ten years. Each issue took as its theme current directions in architecture over the past decade. The theme was the critical look at current directions in architecture and the changes over the last decade. Irrespective of the stylistic considerations, each essay explores a theme in depth, raising most important questions posed by the developing role of architecture.

ESSAYS ON ARCHITECTURE

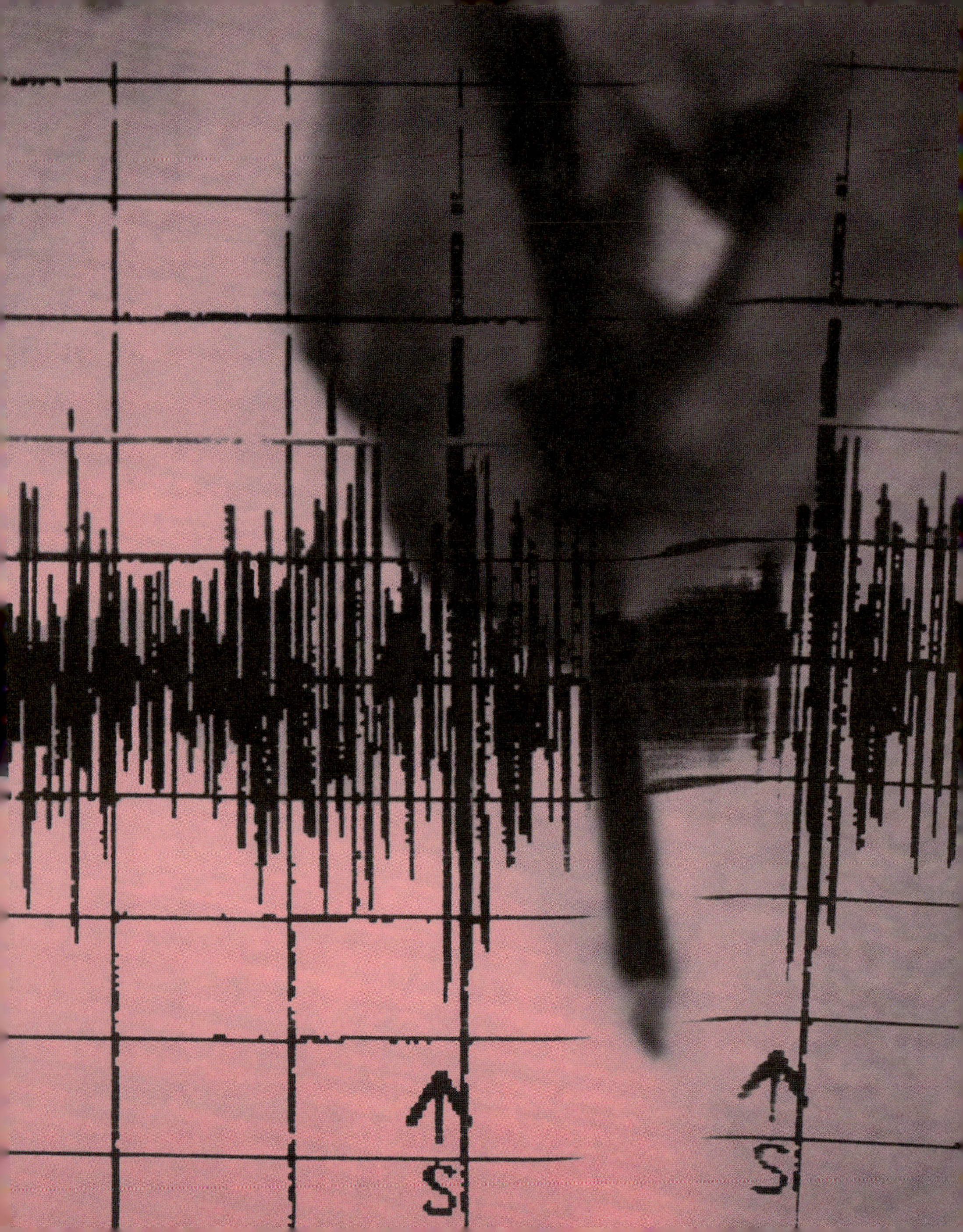
S
S

◄ The Sixth International Architecture Exhibition *Sensing the Future – The Architect as Seismograph*, 1996

HANS HOLLEIN

Sensing the Future:
The Architect as Seismograph

Architects today are the cultural seismographs
of an evolving situation, which they register.
Their work reflects this situation,
projecting it into the future

New Architecture 1: *Reaching for the Future*, 1997

Today there are changing visions of the city; new phenomena are expanding the idea of the city centre, which no longer comprises just a market place, a church, and a town hall. Complex communication systems and new technologies, changing means of transport and advanced methods of construction now determine the planning, development and realization of our environment. A new interpretation of the city's traditional elements and institutions – and the dialectic between city and country – superimposes new concepts on the existing patterns that constitute our understanding of an urban situation.

Both buildings and cities are a result of the efforts of many; and yet single individuals continue to play a leading role in the shaping of our future. Like the other arts and similar disciplines (such as the cinema or politics), architecture has become personalized. It is no longer primarily a matter of movements, of common endeavours based on a dogma, a basic truth or a guiding belief. Rather, new ideas, trends, and visions of the future are now exemplified by the beliefs and work of individuals.

The architect today is anchored in a situation – or creates a situation – in which he acts and to which he reacts, sometimes transgressing the traditional boundaries of "Architecture" while at the same time others become part of "Architecture."

Architects today are the cultural seismographs of an evolving situation, which they register. Their work reflects this situation, projecting it into the future. In their work they do not deal primarily with solving problems but make statements on the potential of architecture – responding to new needs, inventing innovative concepts for a changing way of life, entering new territories, sensing situations as yet unknown.

In all types of buildings – airports, museums, skyscrapers, shopping malls, theatres and sports stadiums, railway stations, fairs, schools, churches and, of course, buildings for working and living in, what is on the drawing board (or in the computer) today is already the real city of the beginning of the next millennium. At this Sixth International Architecture Exhibition of the Venice Biennale, more than seventy architects, planners and artists – roughly divided into the two groups of the seismographic architects with a more established oeuvre and the "emerging voices" – have been invited to present (by means of statements, models, photographs, drawings, videos and other media) some of their most significant recent projects – preferably work realized or under construction – to demonstrate to the public that visions do not necessarily stay on paper but can become reality.

In this context it seems obvious to look back at the articulated forward-looking tendencies of a few decades ago – to the late 1950s, 1960s and early 1970s – when there was a pronounced initiative in various countries concerned with visions of the future, the application of new technologies, a new interpretation of architecture and a blurring of the boundaries between architecture and other disciplines such as art, design, fashion, theatre, literature.

These initiatives were scattered throughout the world but centred on a few specific cities. Their visionary approach had a certain coherence, despite their geographical separation. It was generated by small groups but, with the help of communications, intensified to a world-wide discussion. Radical concepts and fantastic proposals, Utopian visions of the future that were not just theoretical attitudes but called for implementation, came out of London, Vienna, Milan, Tokyo and New York.

There was a glimpse of the future – a future that was perhaps not yet acceptable by society or even technologically possible, but the seismographic sensitivity of this generation and their projects is astounding and worth recalling, so that it can be compared with the tendencies of the emerging voices today and also with current visionary projects and built concepts.

It becomes apparent that yesterday's utopia is today's reality and that many of the visionaries of the 1960s and 1970s are the architects of the recently finished buildings, and of concepts and projects now under construction, which are leading the way into the new millennium.

Address to the Venice Biennale Sixth International Architecture Exhibition
Sensing the Future – The Architect as Seismograph, 1996

Hans Hollein – Volcania, European Centre of Volcanism, model view and detail of cone ▲ ▶

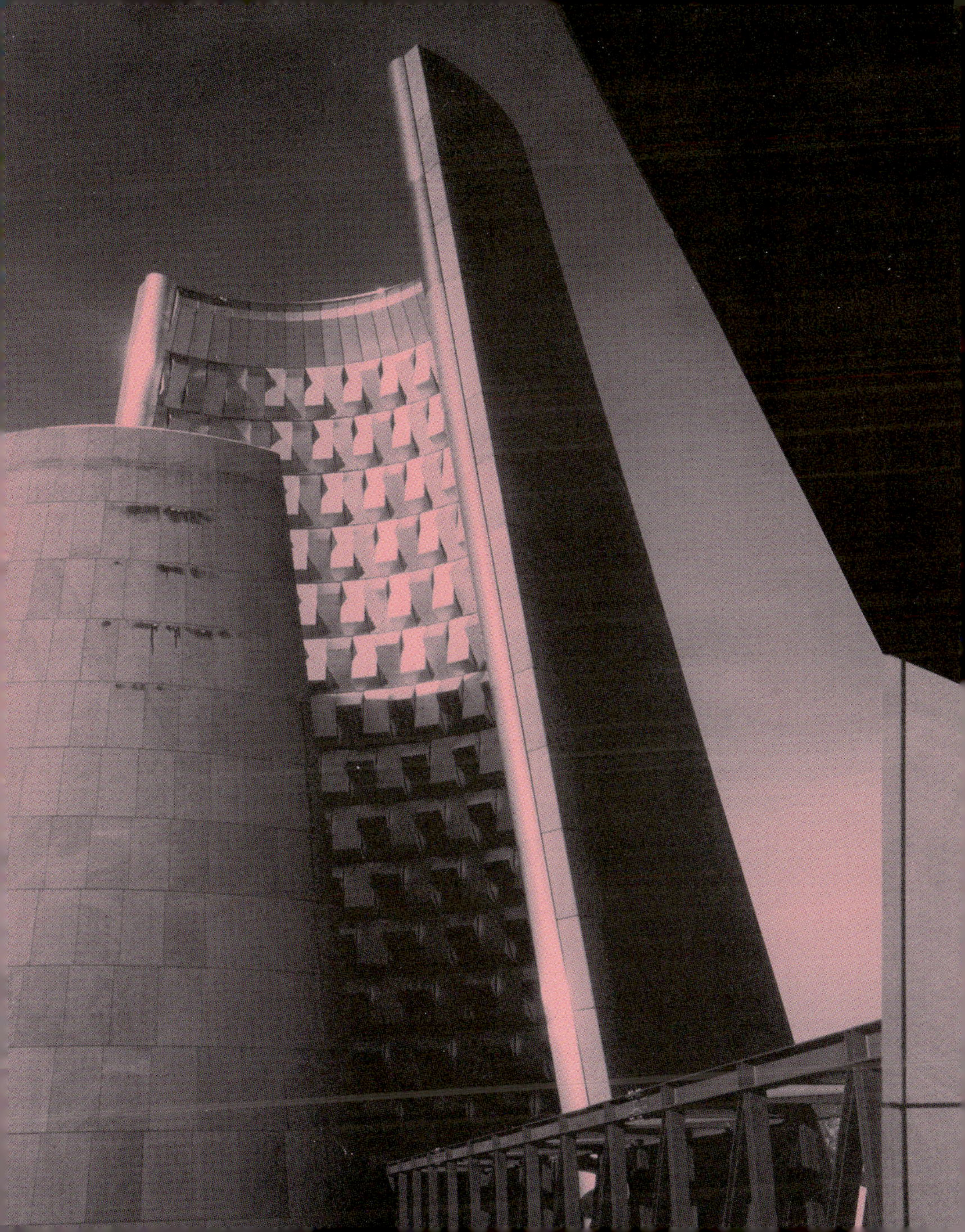

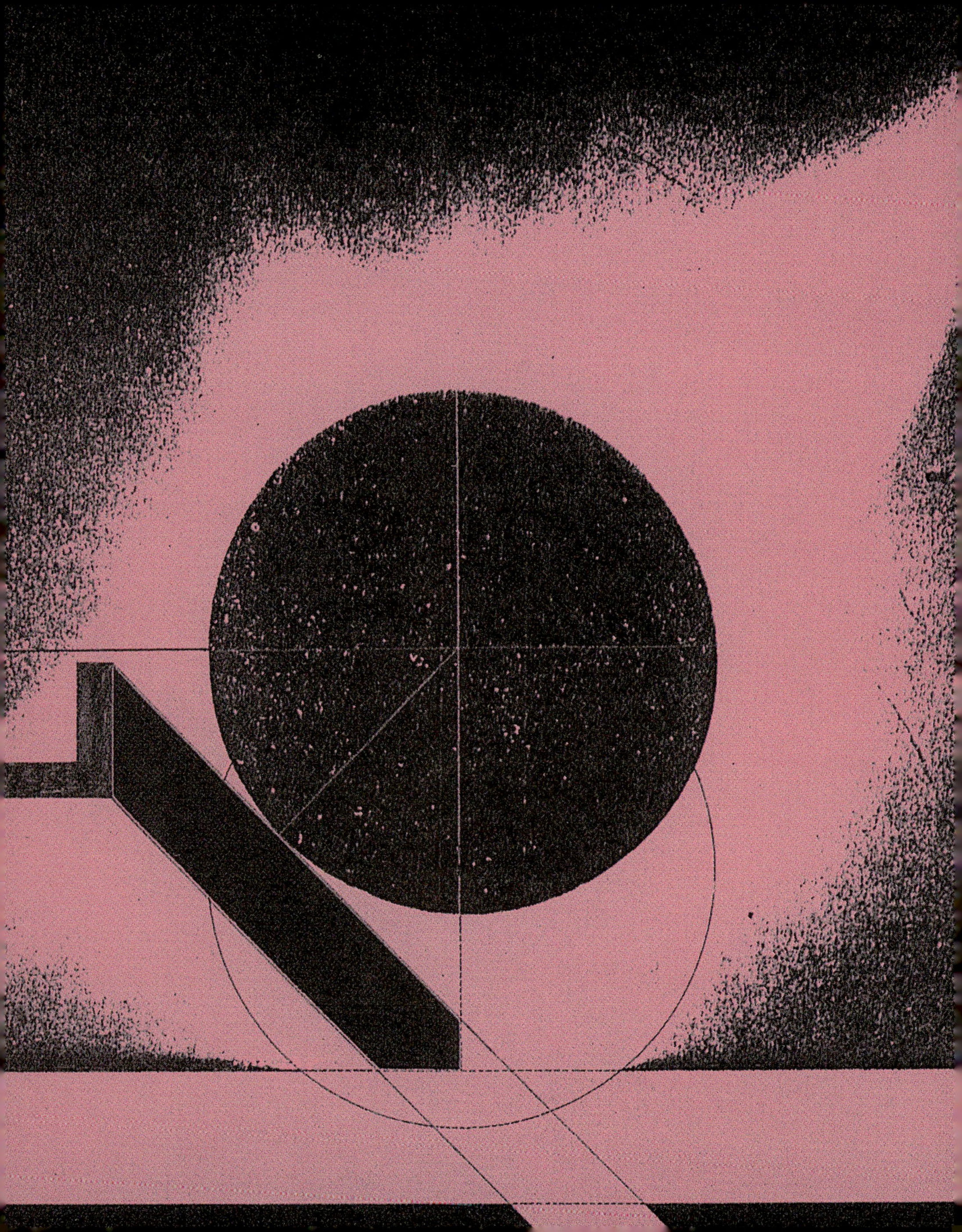

◀ Sketch for Sphere Project for the Museum of Applied Arts, Vienna, 1991

RAIMUND ABRAHAM

Jottings

If architects became aware of the violation involved in digging a hole in the ground and building a building on top of it, they would think twice. And maybe we would have fewer buildings and more architecture

New Architecture 1: *Reaching for the Future*, 1997

It is difficult for students. When I was a student, we had very clearly defined adversaries: our professors were conservative; they believed in a certain kind of typology of buildings and in the comfort of history. And it was very easy to revolt against that. But now you have teachers like me, who encourage students to imagine to their limits and to experiment. The only thing I demand is clarity and discipline. It has become difficult to resist.

○

I practise the discipline of architecture, but I am not a practitioner. I teach architecture but I am not a teacher. I am engaged in theory but I am not a theoretician.

○

When we talk about technology in the context of architecture, we are still talking about a very primitive technology, a technology we can build with, that is based on principles that are thousands of years old. The real technology is the invisible technology of genetic engineering, of microchips and all that. What we are still talking about is a very comfortable technology. But this comfortable technology has one real danger: by its seductive power it can undermine authenticity. In a recent discussion with a friend, I said to him: I am not worried about virtual reality, I worry about virtual authenticity. Virtual reality is simply a consequence of more complicated machines, so anything that is visible or invisible, anything that can be thought of, is real. And so that is not the issue. The issue is that this technology can help us to produce very seductive images, images where buildings appear to be floating, appear to be transparent. And then you ask yourself why?

○

If we expect to make new architecture – and I mean new in the sense of new origins, new originality – then we also have to invent new programmes. We cannot simply accept the old programmes. Habitation is a ritual that is thousands of years old, maybe millions of years old. And we simply have to reinterpret it so that when you say house today, and when you said house a thousand years ago, there is a different programme and I think that is really a necessary sort of challenge that one has to accept in making a new tectonic language. And it Is also in that respect that the technology of our time is leading to an architecture of images.

There were times, short periods of time, when there was collective support for those visions which architects in different parts of the world shared. If you take the historic context of the birth of modern architecture, modern art, there you had a collective breakdown of all social systems – the beginning of the experiment of democracy. That monumental change also produced collective support for a new revolution in the disciplines of the arts. Unfortunately we do not live in a time like that: there is no collective support, and we would be naive to ask for it. The only chance we have is to be as radical as individuals as we can. I have been telling that to my students for thirty years. This is the only freedom we have.

You can never blame; you cannot blame your parents for your failures; you cannot blame the circumstances in which you make your architecture. You have to have the courage to do your own thing. And you see, thinking is dangerous, imagining is even more dangerous. When you go to kindergarten, at a certain point all children are equally imaginative. They all make wonderful paintings and drawings. And then the teacher comes and says: the tree is not blue, it's green, and the sky is blue not red. And so, out of twenty kids there will be maybe three kids who say, "No, my tree is blue." And you can imagine the ratio succumbing to the pressure of authority. When they get to elementary school, to high school, to university, there are very few left, not because they don't have imagination but because they have abandoned it.

○

Radical in my opinion means that you honestly pursue your own limits and the limits of the discipline you are trying to express. Each of us has to do it in her or his own way and I think that is radical. What is not radical goes with the fashion, goes with the trends. Lamenting the lack of support we get, collectively or otherwise, is not radical.

○

When I talk about the origins of architecture, I am not talking about the origins of buildings because there are much older roots than buildings in architecture. And I want to go beyond the roots.

○

A horizon is a phenomenon that is not physical. It is produced by a collision of the cosmological dimensions of our world, of the heavens and the earth. And the horizon belongs neither to the heavens nor to the earth. And so the slightest change on that horizon is a violation of the site. I believe if architects – I would prefer to call them builders – became aware of the violation involved in digging a hole in the ground and building a building on top of it, they would think twice. And maybe we would have fewer buildings and more architecture.

Jottings is taken from an informal public discussion during the Jerusalem Seminar on *Technology, Place and Architecture*, 1996

International Building Exhibition Berlin: Residential and Commercial Building, Friedrichstrasse 32-33, Berlin 1980/87 – Tectonic structure (model) ▶

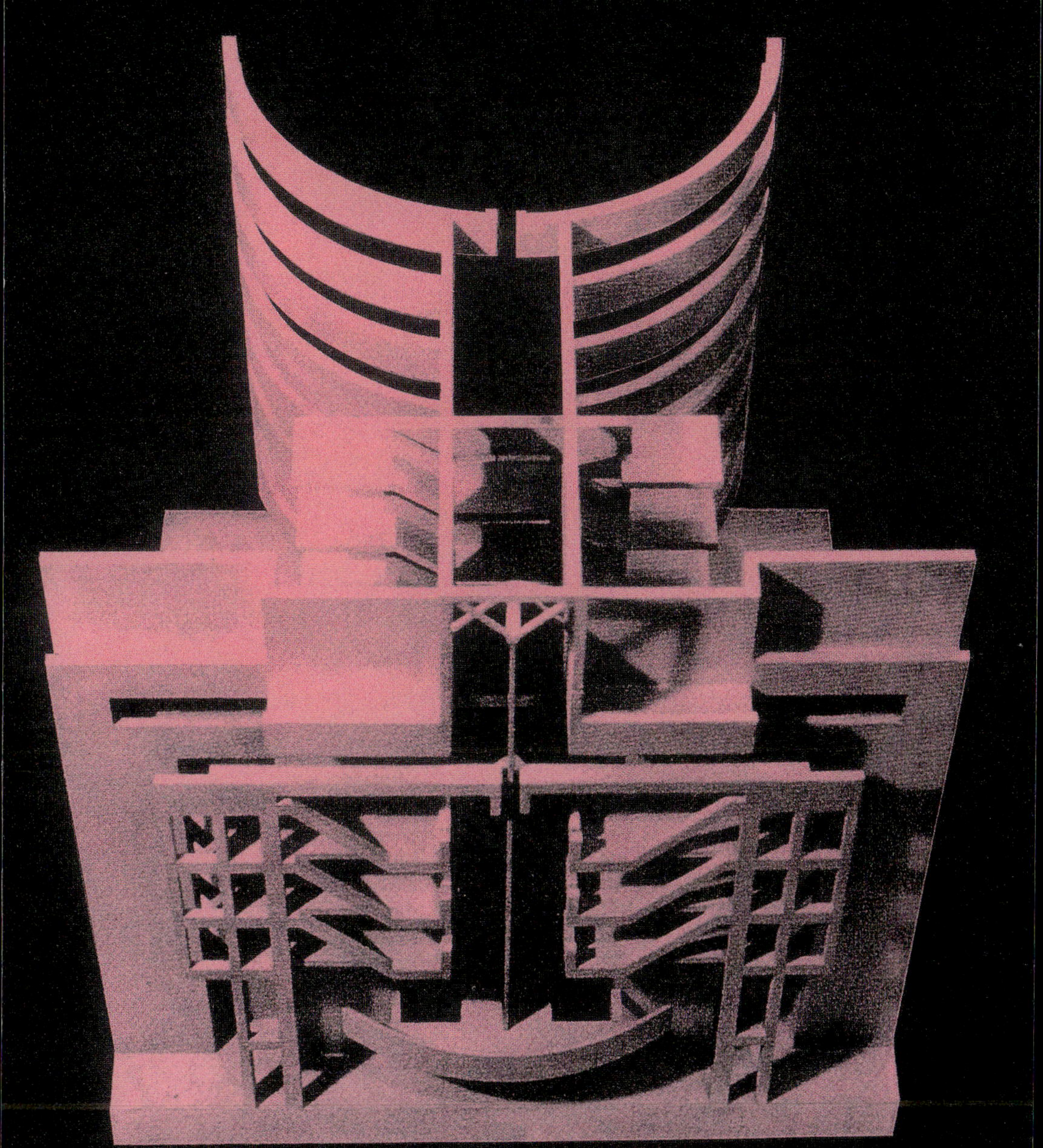

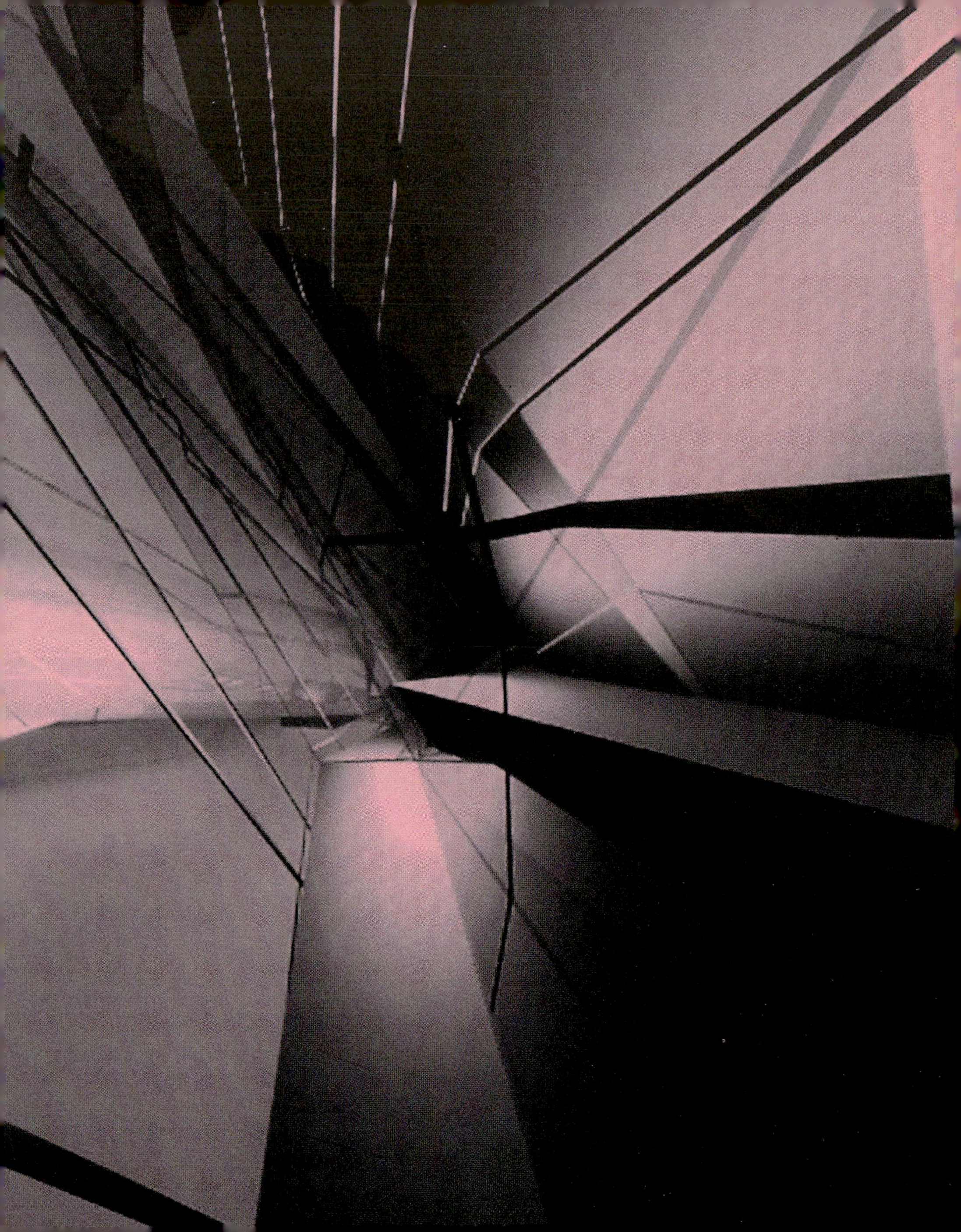

◀ Church of the Year 2000, Rome – view

PETER EISENMAN

Presentness and the "Being-Only-Once" of Architecture

When Vitruvius, in his famous dicta on architecture, used the term 'firmitas', he did not mean that buildings should stand up but rather that they should look like they stand up

New Architecture 1: *Reaching for the Future*, 1997

In her book, *The Optical Unconscious*, Rosalind Krauss discusses a Jackson Pollock painting in relationship to its position in space. She contends that when a Pollock painting is placed in a horizontal position, that is, on the floor as it was painted, it is a "savage work." But the moment the canvas is taken off of the floor and moved to a vertical position on the wall, Krauss continues, it becomes "naturalized," re-institutionalized and re-inscribed into the discourse of painting. All of this is said with an uncharacteristic innocence about the possible effect of the floor or the wall on this change in perception. She assumes that one can lift things up and down, off and on, without any discussion of why the relationship between floor or wall, or, for that matter, between the floor or the wall and the painting, could cause this to happen. What is clear in Krauss's argument is that the contexts provided by architecture, in this case the floor and the wall, do affect how the subject conceptualizes a painting. Yet the issue of how or why such an effect is possible is not discussed. Such an omission is by no means unique to Krauss's argument. Most of those outside of architecture assume that architectural conventions have a thought-to-be naturalness with respect to such things as walls and floors. Jacques Derrida even points out that we must be wary of the idea that architecture "is destined for habitation," that the concept of architecture is "a heritage which comprehends us even before we could submit it to thought." Walter Benjamin also attempts to explain this idea of "destined for

> The concept of architecture is "a heritage which comprehends us even before we could submit it to thought"
>
> *Jacques Derrida*

habitation" in a different way. He says, "In architecture, habit determines to a large extent even optical reception. Architecture cannot be understood by optical means alone, that is by contemplation. It is mastered gradually by habit." Thus in one sense the wall is already seen in any specific context by habit. This could be responsible for the naturalizing of the Pollock painting, since it is known that all paintings by force of habit are hung on walls and not on floors. Clearly, the question of habit and the habitual is already predetermined when dwellings are called places of habitation, as opposed to say places of occupation. But this assumption of habit alone, it will be argued here, is not enough to account for the naturalizing effect of the wall on the Pollock painting. Nor can the ideas of an a *priori* destiny or naturalness, the assumption that "this is the way things are," be the only cause of this effect. Clearly something else must be at work. And it is this something else that makes architecture a problematic discourse.

The very conditions that bring about this idea of an a *priori* destiny or a thought to be naturalness of architecture, and thus what makes architecture problematic, lie initially in the fact that architecture is alone of all the discourses in its particular linking of its iconicity with its instrumentality, its meaning with its objecthood. A wall in architecture is not merely holding something up, it also symbolizes that act of holding up. Architecture, Derrida says, "cannot be without meaning." One cannot have the wall without the sign of the wall and vice versa; architecture will always implicate the wall. When Vitruvius, in his famous dicta on architecture, used the term *firmitas*, he did not mean that buildings should stand up (since all buildings of necessity must stand up) but rather that they should look like they stand up. It has been argued that in all disciplines instrumentality in some way affects iconicity; for example, the form of a book, its pagination, type, and binding, all affect our reading of the text, but not all texts are necessarily in book form. Yet in architecture there will always be the presence of walls, walls that are both icon and instrument. It is this unique linkage that becomes problematic, because in order to "deconstruct" the meaning of architecture, one must attempt to separate the presence of the wall from the meaning of the wall – what in fact cannot be separated. Thus, unlike any other discourse, architecture both resists and requires the deconstructive impulse. This resistance alone should be of interest to deconstructive thought.

In addition to the strong connection between iconicity and instrumentality, architecture also has a unique relationship to what Jacques Derrida refers to in *The Truth in Painting* as the "once only" of a work of art. The condition of this "once only" at work in architecture is not the same as in painting or in photography. Derrida poses the issue of the "being-only-once" of a work of art as the fault line of deconstruction in its relationship to painting and photography. He cites Walter Benjamin, and says, "As soon as the technique of reproduction reaches the stage of photography a break line and also a new front traverses the whole space of art. The presumed uniqueness of production, the "being-only-once" of the exemplar and the value of authenticity, is practically deconstructed." Therefore it could be argued that the work of deconstruction has as one of its objects the notion of the displacement of the original, the prior condition of either a painting or a photograph.

In terms of photography, the "being only once" formerly devolved upon the issue of the original photographic plate in relation to the serial print. The plate is manipulated in development to produce a serial work, which bears the mark of the hand of the author as well as that of the process. For example, a photograph can be developed with more or less grain, more or less contrast, and more or less light and intensity. Under these circumstances, the value of the photographic object relies both on the quality of the original plate and the quality of the reproduction as well as the limited seriality of the reproduction. The number one-often is of more value to a collector than the number two-of-ten. There is a prior value given to the closeness of the copy in time to the plate which in this case is the being-only-once. The use of the plate and the collection of the plate – whether plates are destroyed or not – defines the problematic of originality in the era of mechanical reproduction.

When one moves from the mechanical paradigm to the electronic paradigm another issue enters in. Conditions are no longer the same for the photograph. (It should be noted that for the sake of this argument only the question of replication in photography and not in painting is at issue.) The possibility of an electronically reproduced photograph becomes interesting in this context as it represents the ultimate deconstruction of the original. Now, instead of a plate, a physical negative, there are only electronic impulses, ones and zeroes – impulses of light. The object no longer contains being, but only exists as contiguous electronic impulses; there is no longer a being-only-once. This erasure of the being-only-once that is proposed by the digitized photograph has several consequences. At one and the same time, it turns the mediation that was present in the photograph from a condition of self-similarity to self-sameness. For it is possible to digitize a photograph in such a way as to reproduce it so that even an expert cannot tell if it was the first instance or the second. In digitized reproduction the self-same characteristic is so strong that it is impossible to discern the difference even with a so-called expert mediating eye. In other words, all of the potential subjective characteristics of the being-only-once are erased. But equally, the converse is true.

> In order to "deconstruct" the meaning of architecture, one must attempt to separate the presence of the wall from the meaning of the wall – what in fact cannot be separated

Formerly, one was able to trust a photograph for documentary evidence. For example if one wanted to buy a Rembrandt, verifying that the Rembrandt was authenticated by a signature could be done through a photograph. Therefore, a self-same photograph would become the most objective record that one could have. But the digitized photograph – the new self-same record – is now most open to mediation, and thus to being manipulated. It is possible to change a photograph of an original painting, an original that did not have a Rembrandt signature, by putting in such a signature without anyone being able to detect that the photograph has been doctored. It would thus appear that the evidence originally there was in fact not. In the digitizing process two things happen. First, there is a collapse of the idea of the being-only-once as the idea of the original or the authentic, and second, the role of the hand of the author, which formerly was a distinguishing characteristic between an objectifying and a subjectifying process, also becomes blurred. These two processes become, as it were, superimposed over one another; time and space as the limits of difference are erased. In fact, it can be argued that they deconstruct one another because there is no longer the possibility that the photograph can be relied on for objective truth. But equally the digitized photograph does not bear any trace of its process, and thus it is no longer possible to tell if there was any authorial mediation. In fact, the digitized photograph becomes simultaneously subject to the most mediation and to the least mediation.

> Often times the drawing of architecture is more of an original than the work of architecture: as when Palladio redraws all of his buildings as they were designed to be, rather than as they were built

This produces a condition whereby the mediation of the author is seen within a different spectrum. It either takes place, at the one end, as the traditional art object, with its value in presence, or, at the other, as the nihilistic gesture of the erasure of the object and the authorial trace. This spectrum of discourse, it can be argued, is only possible in print media – that is, where the possibility of repetition and replication is at issue. This is not the case with architecture.

The discourse of replication, and thus the question of the original, would seem not to be at issue in built architecture.

That a building is always a unique instance would be the argument of conventional wisdom. But before this can be assumed, one must first put aside the unique relationship that built work has to its drawing (which in its more general consequences is a broader issue that will not be discussed here). Oftentimes the drawing of architecture is more of an original than the work of architecture: as when Palladio redraws all of his buildings as they were designed to be, rather than as they were built; or when Daniel Libeskind in his Micromegas Project draws an architecture that is not intended to be built; or when Piranesi draws, in his *Carceri* series, architectures that could never be built. In each of these examples the drawing of architecture becomes an original instance, and thus questions the simplistic view of building as an example of a being-only-once. But it is not the instance of building that is intended here as the reference for this unique being-only-once of architecture. While in one sense the built work in its site and programmatic specificity is always a unique instance, this is once again an overly determined answer, and one that does not speak to a condition which can be considered unique in architecture.

Derrida himself comes closer to refining this unique condition when he says that architecture is more like the idea of an event, which "reinvents architecture in a series of 'only onces' which are always unique in their repetition." This idea overlays replication with the idea of the unique, that architecture can be replicated, and that this replication is always unique. This quality of the unique is brought about by the fact that architecture always demands presence. While it is possible to challenge the idea of the presence of an object with regard to works of photography, and clearly to works of other written, mediated discourses on tape or on film, it is not as simple to challenge in architecture.

While deconstruction seems to take into consideration the idea that architecture, unlike painting and photography, is a highly conventionalized

PETER EISENMAN

system; and while it may be possible to loosen architecture's relationship to its instrumentality, that is to loosen the relationship between form and function, it is impossible to deny architecture's metaphysics of presence. Even in a condition of virtual reality, architecture is conventionalized as the metaphysics of presence; within virtual reality, architecture is still imagined as a physical body. It is this metaphysics of presence that dominates any discussion of architecture. Therefore in order to propose a deconstruction of architecture it is necessary to propose something that can overcome this dominance of presence.

It will be argued here that this unique conventionality of architecture, which links its iconicity and instrumentality, already contains the capacity to open up and separate its condition of presence from its meaning. This opening up creates a possibility for another condition of being-only-once. That is, once the separation of the thought to be natural and normative conditions of architecture is proposed, there is the possibility of another being-only-once, which can be seen as the opposite of the deconstruction of the being-only-once in painting. And it is the deconstruction of this natural relationship that puts into place another being-only-once that is unique to architecture. This condition can be properly called *presentness*.

Presentness can be defined in several different ways. First, the term should not be confused with Michael Fried's use of a term with the same name. According to Rosalind Krauss, presentness for Fried is a "reinscribing of modernism within a historic metaphysics." For Fried, presentness was a moment which collapsed time into the inexorable present, where there was no difference between thinking and experience. For Derrida, experience is something outside of, or different from, this time frame. The event for Derrida, i.e. the time frame of the moment, requires the "writing of a space," a mode of spacing which distinguishes the space of the event from the time of the event. My use of the term *presentness* also begins from an idea of spacing, a spacing which is required in the loosening of the relationship of the architectural object from its thought to be a natural condition of instrumentality. Thus, in one sense, *presentness*, as I conceive it, is precisely the opposite of the Fried definition. As Krauss points out, the central concept of the phenomenology of self-presence requires an undivided unity of a temporal present, that is, between the object and the sign. Precisely because this relationship is so predetermined in architecture, the term presentness offers a means to loosen the inexorable relationship of the architectural object from its thought to be natural condition of instrumentality.

If *presentness* is such an occupied term, why the insistence on its use? More than any other term it combines both the idea of time in presence, of the experience of space in the present, while at the same time its *suffixness* causes a distance between the object as presence, which is a given in architecture, and the quality of that presence as time, which may be something other than mere presence. This creates the idea of a spacing between presence and the quality of presentness. However, this does not in any way implicate two other characteristics of presentness: that is its quality of an already given, and its capacity to render that already given as necessarily subversive. These latter two characteristics, unique to architecture, also distinguish *presentness* from Derrida's use of the term *maintenant* which in many respects may be seen as similar. *Maintenant*, while implicating both time and space in its idea of maintaining, does not demand the quality of subversion as a prior condition to any transformation, which it is argued here is a necessary condition of architecture. It is precisely the subversion of the type and the norm, of the thought to be natural relationship between icon and instrument that creates architecture's being-only-once. As long as the instrumentality of architecture is seen to be its form and its function –

> As long as the instrumentality of architecture is seen to be its form and its function, and as long as this thought to be natural condition is seen as a two-term system, it represses the possibility of presentness

whether that function is its site, programme, or structure, and its form is its aesthetic, style, or iconography – and as long as this thought to be natural condition is seen as a two-term system, it represses the possibility of presentness.

The importance of presentness as a term for architecture is that it distinguishes a writing from an instrumentality of aesthetics and meaning. Presentness as a writing is the possibility of a subversion of the thought to be convention of type in architecture; that architecture has within it an insidedness which is an already existing possibility for the subversive. Presentness is both the possibility of, if not the need for, architecture to stabilize itself through the reabsorption of the transformation of type brought about by this subversion, and simultaneously the resistance to this reabsorption. This insidedness as a writing is both a trace of this already given and the possibility to experience this trace in space. Trace is the possibility of the subversion of a primordial type, which itself is constantly being over time, to become at any given time in the history of architecture, the then existing convention of type. To achieve this subversion, architecture must always overcome the normative typological and social gestures

While [Ronchamp] only contained a presentness of the new, that is, that it was theatrical and performative, it did nothing to displace the instrumentality of type in the notion of the church

that, at any given time, attempt to maintain its status quo. Architecture only continues and maintains itself precisely because of this subversive impulse to produce its being-only-once. For example, in *Michelangelo's Laurentian Library* there is a subversion of the type form of the then existing library type. Because to this day this subversion has not been absorbed into the library type, that is, the library type has not transformed itself to include the subversion of the more general type manifest in the specific instance of presentness in the Laurentian Library, it still retains the same effective charge, the presentness of its being-only-once that it had in the sixteenth century. Thus, while part of this idea of presentness obviously deals with the condition of the new, and the time of the new, it also deals with the time of duration, that is with the subversion of presence as trace. Clearly when Michelangelo subverted the type-form of the library in his Laurentian project, it was a subversion also of the existing style of architecture, and in that sense it was also new. The fact that today one experiences this duration of presentness (and this is a condition of experience and not so much of drawing) means that the subversion has been a continuous one that has not been absorbed into the conventional instrumentality of architecture.

This idea of presentness as a being-only-once unique to architecture, that is, as a subversion of type, can also be seen if one takes two late projects by Le Corbusier, the chapel at Ronchamp and the monastery at La Tourette, both of which contained at the time of their building a presentness. It could be argued that Ronchamp only contained a presentness of the new, that is, that it was theatrical and performative. While it affected experience because of its newness, it did nothing to displace the instrumentality of type in the notion of the church. It is precisely the theatricality of the gestures of Ronchamp that have been reabsorbed in architecture, so that today the presentness of Ronchamp is no longer what it was. However, at La Tourette, a monastery, presentness was brought about by the subversion of both type form and icon. There was a new idea of what it was to be a monastery. At La Tourette this condition of presentness remains in place today because the dislocation of the type has not been reabsorbed in the conventional idea of the monastery type. It still remains a displacement, a subversion of the condition of the type that had formally existed. This same idea could also be argued in my own work, for example in the Wexner Center in Columbus, Ohio, and in the Convention Center in the same city. The Wexner Center is an example of presentness precisely because it subverts the instrumentality and iconicity of the museum, whereas the Columbus Convention Center is more theatrical and does not involve the subversion of type (in fact, it involves the maintenance of type), and therefore will be less articulate in the future as a condition of presentness.

If architecture is a unique condition of discourse where the sign and the signified are more closely linked than in any other discourse, presentness is a way of opening up what is repressed in the assumed to be natural instrumentality of form and function, or of meaning and function. Presentness requires the constant subversion of this instrumentality in order to write an architecture as a trace of presence within presence. This becomes particularly critical within the terms of an electronic paradigm, where the former boundaries that maintained any discourse are blurred. As in contemporary physics and biology, where the hegemony of cause and effect has been undermined, so too the cause and effect of architecture, form and function, presence and absence, could be opened up by a condition of presentness.

Architecture can neither merely return to a dialectic of the metaphysics of presence nor return to a nihilism which denies presence. Presentness is an alternative term that does not force a choice between these two. It could be argued that, since presentness is an already given of architecture, it has always been potentially active in the problematic of architecture but, because of the bond between icon and instrument has tended to be repressed by them. It could further be argued that the simultaneous resistance and requirement of an architecture to the idea of a being-only-once would allow deconstruction to think its discourse through architecture in a way that it could not in other modes of being. This would allow one to say that architecture, in its resistance to deconstruction, also requires deconstruction, and that architecture provides a space different from the space of language, literature, or painting, that could be an affective means for deconstruction to rethink itself today.

Church of the Year 2000, Rome – view ▶

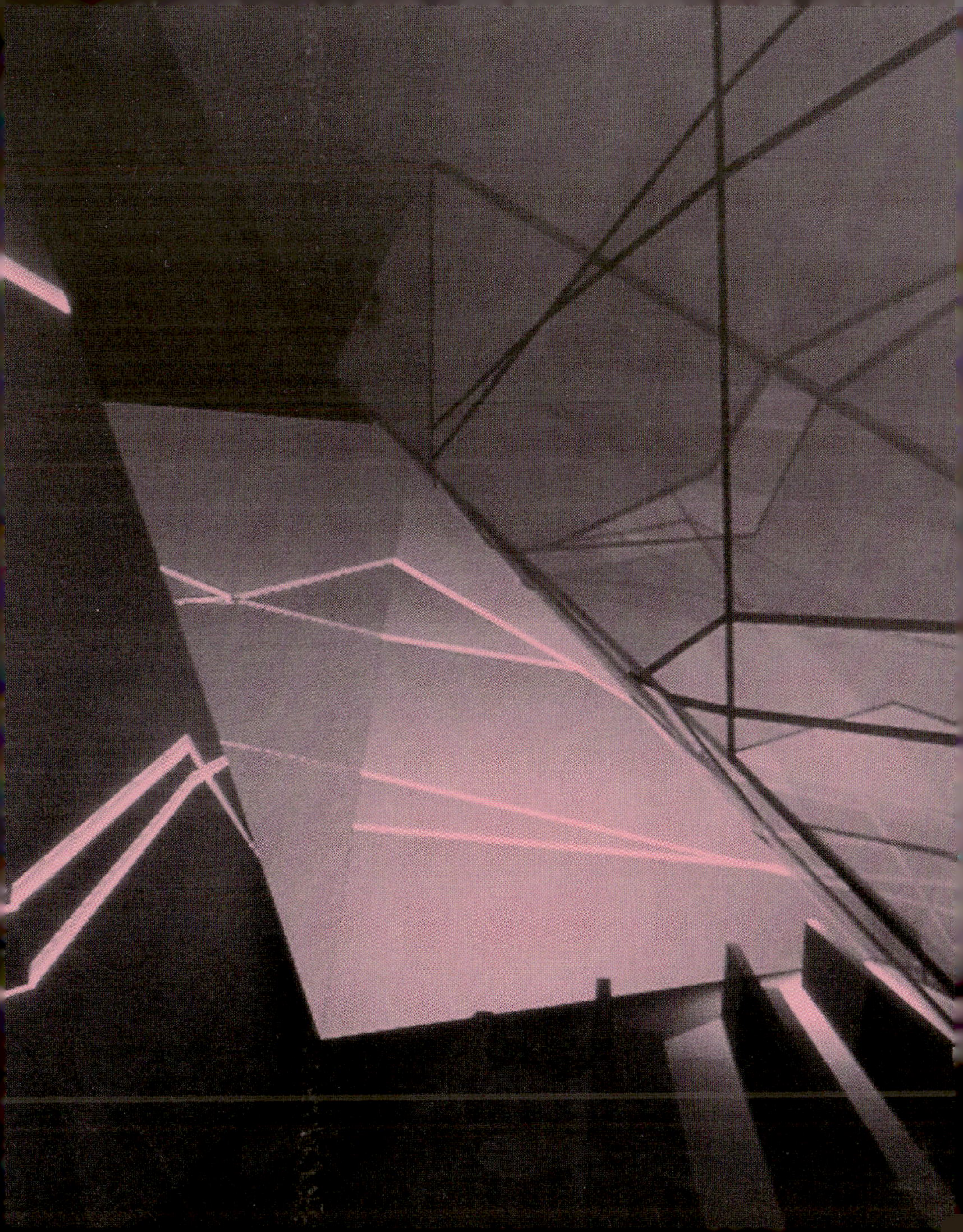

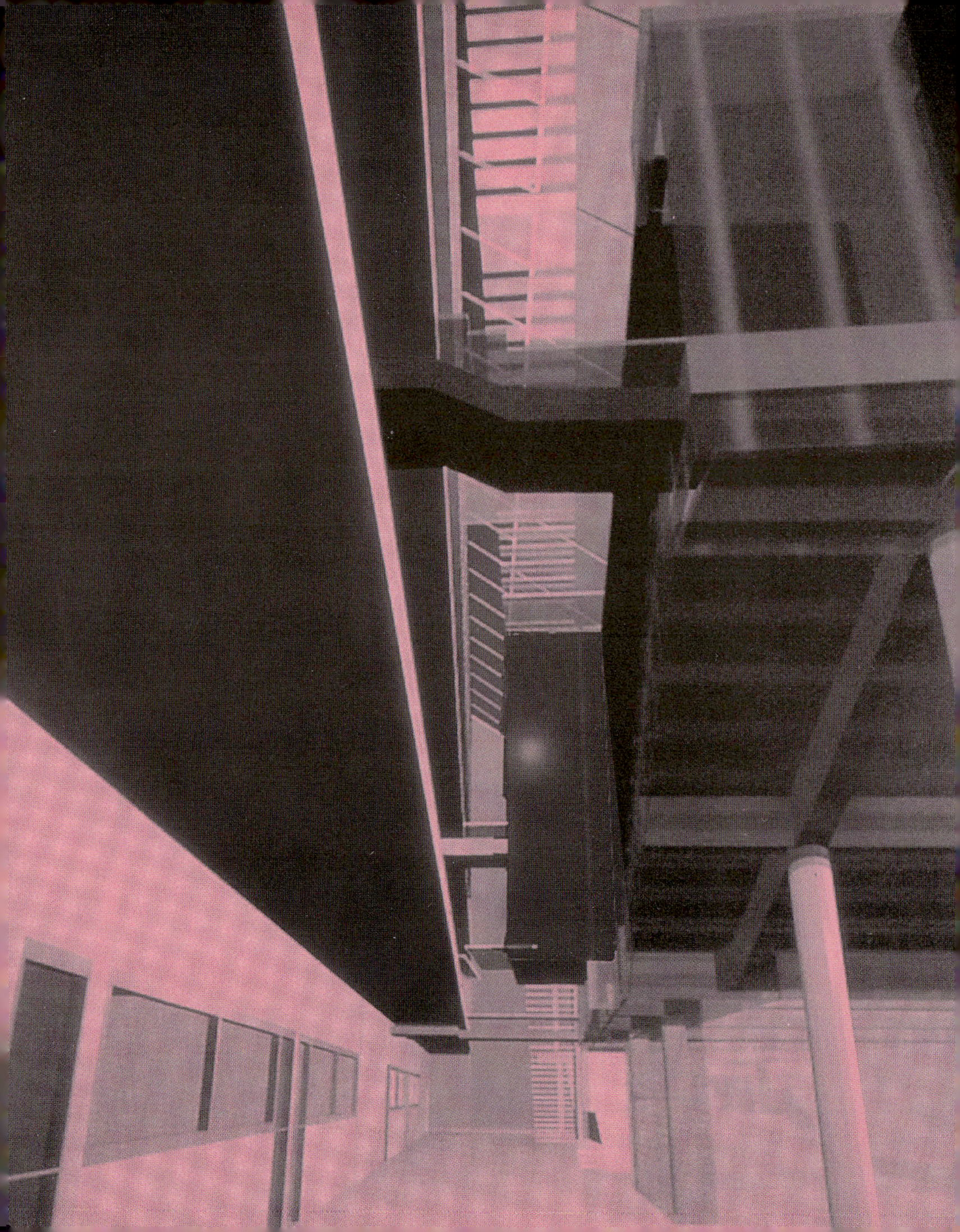

◀ School of Architecture, Marne-la-Vallée, France – view looking west between amphitheatre and north blocks

BERNARD TSCHUMI

Architecture and Events

We are not dealing with a homogeneous space but with a space that is always in question through movement or use

New Architecture 1: *Reaching for the Future*, 1997

I shall attempt to define complexity in architecture. Not complexity in the sense of the complexity and contradiction of Venturi, but rather the complexity in architecture that seeks to take account of the concept of programme and the concept of movement as the basis for any definition. I shall do this by discussing a certain number of projects.

I constantly travel between the United States and France and there is a sort of duality from this toing and froing between two very different cultures, American culture and European culture – and here I am going beyond architecture to everything from across the Atlantic that has contributed to culture in Europe through the cinema, through a certain form of art and thought; and all the work on theory, and the work based on philosophy and literature that has enriched European thought. And, curiously, this starting point for the joining of the two cultures is very important because it is also the starting point for a sort of heterogeneity that has no place in the Modernist canon of architecture. It is not static, unitary thought, but rather conceptual coherence that takes as its starting point a dynamic of incoherence and discontinuity.

What is the starting point for architecture? One of the arguments was that architecture is above all an event and not form

When we had an exhibition at the Museum of Modern Art in New York entitled *Architecture and Event* we thought that it would be a quiet exhibition that would perhaps go unnoticed, but curiously it proved to be a very polemic exhibition. It was well received in architectural circles but severely criticized by one important broad-circulation newspaper. Why? Perhaps because it was designed around the question of programme not form. What is a programme? What is the starting point for architecture? One of the arguments of the exhibition was that architecture is above all an event and not form. This seemed to pose a problem, to provoke questions. Of course, there was a context – the context of our work – that is related to what has happened in other fields: in conceptual art at a certain time, and then, obviously, the cinema, which is fascinating because it relates to both space and action at the same time.

There was a time when I was involved in the creation of a number of advertisements for architecture – before I entered competitions and before I attempted to build – in which the major premise was that there is no architecture without an event; that there is no space without action. And, by extension, that there is no space without violence. And, in this sense, it was an anti-formal discourse. Anti-form as a generator of architecture: a way of looking at architecture as a series of more or less autonomous manipulations or transformations but always linked to the concept of the event. And so the exhibition at MoMA wanted to be in suspense, shifting; it sought to show that our architecture was not an architecture of certainties but an architecture that always posed questions.

Obviously, the first question deals with the definition of architecture. In a work begun in the mid 1970s entitled *The Manhattan Transcripts*, one hypothesis seemed absolutely obvious to me: architecture is action, space and movement at the same time. What is built is not a partial component of architecture. Whence a tripartite notation system based on the principle that in architecture plans, perspectives and sections are very sophisticated means of presentation that have led to extraordinary results; but, at the same time, they are a method of unfinished notation. Perhaps what was needed in architecture was to find a means of notation closer to that other definition of architecture, which is the definition of the programme, of the event. The plan, of course, but also the movement of the body in space.

"Event, a disparate multiplicity." This definition of architecture is both a dynamic and a static definition in the sense that we are not dealing with a homogeneous space but with a space that is always in question through movement or use. At that time (we are still speaking about work done twenty years ago), my starting-point was scenarios or rather images from strips of film. On the basis of the movement of the various protagonists I tried to draw spaces that corresponded to their movements, rather like the tradition started by Oscar Schlemmer at the Bauhaus: it is the movement of the body in space that determines the space and, in practice, creates it. And so this creation of the vector of movement was a very strong starting point, just as it is in the films of Hitchcock, the films of Griffith – *The Birth of a Nation* – those of Welles and others who are seeking some kind of architectural formulation. The same question was being posed in literary texts. When a contractor gives you a programme, it often emanates from certain cultural *a priori*. And so the starting point here was: if there are cultural *a priori*, we may as well look for them directly in a novel or a story. We can just as well look in Calvino as in Hegel.

Another example is the work done by my students at the Architectural Association in London with James Joyce as the starting point. That allowed us, via a pinpoint grid – which gave rise to the pinpoint grid of La Villette – to say: we shall take certain points in Joyce's text and try and develop a combination of architectural elements that are associated in a similar way to Joyce's play on words. Of course, later this will all be linked to deconstruction – a term that we are now somewhat afraid to use since it became so famous in the United States after the 1988 exhibition at the MoMA, but also perhaps because of the way of qualifying as 'deconstructed' anything that is abstract or fragmented. In fact, what we were doing was to study the combination of space and movement in the most objective way possible.

For example, in our project at Kassel for Documenta, the roofs of the buildings and the different elements are literally deconstructed – it is very literal indeed in this particular case – and put back in place, reconstructed, recomposed, reformed, but according to rules and tools that are, of course, very different from traditional composition because my work is never based on composition but on either the materialization of the concepts of the programme or on vectors of movement; it either combines or reorganizes, or perhaps assembles; but it is never a composition.

Architecture is action, space and movement at the same time

To conclude this introduction on the definition of architecture, I shall return to *The Manhattan Transcripts*, four episodes in a sort of architectural detective story that took as its framework four urban archetypes in Manhattan: the park (Central Park), the street (42nd Street), the tower (a sky-scraper), and a city block. Systematically, we find the principle of tripartite composition where the upper section provides the architectural spaces; the second line is the line of movement, arrows, vectors (here they come from a game, American football), which are given material form in a series of walls, passages, ramps, and corridors. And then, of course, the action, the event: the manipulation of these different aspects of what architecture might be – event, space and movement – to create architecture without any hierarchy whatsoever, without at any moment saying that one of these criteria is more important than another. What we are saying is: here is a definition of architecture that is somewhat indecisive; it is not possible to give priority to one aspect of architecture over another, to what is built or to what happens inside what is built.

We should look at some examples of real building for an explanation. First, the glass video gallery in Groningen in the north of Holland. The programme was a programme for a video and music festival for which a certain number of architects created pavilions throughout the city, to give some protection to spectators while they watched music and video films. Our approach consisted in the first place of an inversion. We decided that we would make our pavilion entirely of glass – a sort of space for peeping Toms. But we refused the hierarchy of a metallic structure filled with glass since today structural glass permits the use of both glass beams and glass pillars.

In this pavilion the whole structure is glass. The space is at a slight angle, sloping on both the vertical and the horizontal to try and avoid any relation with gravity because we were dealing above all with images that established themselves through the showing of different films; and to do it in such a way that the definition of the space would go beyond the Modernist definition of the glass house. By glass house I do not mean Chareau's, but those of Mies van der Rohe or Johnson where, if you take away the glass, the metal structure and the roof plan remain completely defining the space. But if you take away the glass from the pavilion in Groningen, nothing remains; the structure itself is held together with clips – a pun, of course – but that is not important. What we were attempting to do was to create an immaterial architecture that would be materialized by an event, by use, by the programme. At night the transformation is unbelievable: it is like a hall of mirrors – the video screens are duplicated ad infinitum in every direction and, in addition, the angle completely changes the relation to the body.

Here is a definition of architecture that is somewhat indecisive; it is not possible to give priority to one aspect of architecture over another, to what is built or to what happens inside what is built

And so this is one starting point for the definition of architecture through the programme. It poses an interesting question: if you do not submit passively to the demands of the programmers, how can you extend the concept of programme so that once it is combined with architecture, it becomes a generator of events?

In the case of our competition entry for the Très Grande Bibliothèque in Paris, the invention was a running track that crossed the reading room. It was, in fact, a very realist project but a bit like a manifesto. We said to ourselves: there is always a crossroads, interpenetration between movement and space; and this led to the runners across the library. But it is also the principal moment of the project, the point where invention comes into play. It states: here is the building system – in this case a system of triangular *caissons* and bearer beams in partial suspension – which underlines the concept of the architecture and the programme.

Another example of this relationship between the concept and the building system is the competition entry, for which we won second prize, for Kansaï airport near Osaka in Japan. In this case, we reformulated a programme for transfers from plane to train to create a sort of linear city, an in-between city inserted between the elements of the official programme. And so we wrote a second programme, in addition to the required programme, that stated: since today, at the end of the twentieth century, airports are probably the most vital of things, together with, of course, computers and microchips, perhaps there is a way we can take advantage of this in-between, of this non-programmed space within which we propose a new city, a linear city in the tradition of the linear cities of Malta i Soria, Leonidov and Le Corbusier. And so we have a project where the very particular structure (the deformation of a slanted sinusoid) plays the role of generator of a city. In short, a new 'parasite' programme, inserted in gaps in the official programme gave rise to an urban event. The place where we went beyond the official programme became the place of invention.

The next project is Le Fresnoy, an arts centre in Tourcoing, France. Here, there is an attempt at interdisciplinarity but what it in fact wants to do is to sweep away all categories; it is not the Bauhaus, it is not a way of serializing or categorizing knowledge. It is not a matter of saying that on one side we have painting, on the other dance, then sculpture, then architecture; it is much more a place of exchange where one discipline – for example, sculpture – is affected by the electronic image, the cinema, etc. For the past five or seven years, the organizers of numerous competitions have referred to the electronic Bauhaus, but without any serious research, the opposite of Le Fresnoy where the programme was of great quality. The starting point was already rather curious: it was not the *tabula rasa* or virgin space of Gropius; but a rather curious building consisting of a series of additions and juxtapositions, built between the 1920s and 1950s, which served as a place for leisure, for meeting people and for dancing. It was the first cinema in northern France but also a place for wrestling and roller skating, where there was a roundabout, and, at certain times, a swimming pool. And so it was a rather surrealist place, in such a bad state of repair that it was about to be demolished, with rather troubling spaces. The roofs were rotten and the scale of the interior spaces Piranesian. We decided that if we created a new building by demolishing the old one, we risked falling into Gropius's trap of seeking certainty in architectural form; whereas we were concerned with contamination, antiform. And so we said: no, there are no absolute forms, there are no preferred forms. Therefore, there was only one unbelievable thing to be done, which was to keep the building. Not to preserve it or to restore it – I never wanted to put this building in the context of restoration because that was secondary – but to put a large umbrella roof that would protect the building from the weather and provide all the services necessary in a contemporary building such as air-conditioning, drainage, etc.

Of course, what was interesting was what would happen between the old roof structure and the new roofs: there would be a space. An immense space, 100m x 100m, a true architectural space, but not in the Bauhaus sense. The space we have achieved is a residual space: it is not composed or designed but is simply the result of the logic of the initial concept of juxtaposition. There is a parallel: on the one hand, an interior perspective of Mies van der Rohe's conference centre dating from the 1950s; and, on the other, a document that Mies calls his 'Concert Hall' dating from about 1942. This concert hall is an industrial space – a hangar – with one or two Miesian paper walls and a Maillol statue; and, right at the back, partly hidden, some bombers. He calls it a 'Concert Hall.' By simply placing an event inside a box that has nothing to do with it, he creates a deviation that places the event, the action, at the centre of the architecture.

> We put new architecture inside existing architecture... to define the architecture as the event. We have used a new envelope with the old buildings inside, like Russian dolls

What we tried to do at Le Fresnoy was to put new architecture inside existing architecture, in other words to define the architecture as the event. We have used a new envelope with the old buildings inside, like Russian dolls. There is a new box inside an old box, for it is obvious that when you have a building in such a bad state, it is necessary to create at least some protected inside space for high technology purposes. This is the 'in-between' space between the old roofs and our new 'electronic' roof, the roof that is the basis of the whole pedagogical and architectural project. It is therefore a residue, a left-over, that uses a third dimension.

Of course we had a programme with detailed specifications on how it would function. But here, there was an opportunity to use this empty space, this left-over space that came free, because it was empty. And so this empty space called for some kind of invention. The whole unconscious element of this project lies in this disassociation and in the in-between space, where artists can create exhibitions, some of their films, and do research into images. A system of footbridges and ramps in this in-between space allows the public in: there is a restaurant and an open-air cinema. This is not the result of the usual dialectic between two elements, but of several texts, several ways of treating the architectural elements and the programme elements to transform them, in similar vein to *The Manhattan Transcripts*, into an architectural event.

My next project continues the theme of the in-between, of the non-programmed space that finds its justification in the large number of activities in the programme: once again we looked for gaps in the programme, the left-over spaces, to understand their effect on the architecture.

Columbia University in New York is a rather exceptional campus almost in the city centre, built by the American architects McKim, Mead and White, one of whom studied at the Ecole des Beaux-Arts in Paris at the end of the nineteenth century; it is a somewhat Palladian composition incorporating a large number of colleges and departments – there are almost 20,000 students at present – and a structure defined by a monumental foundation wall around a platform on which the buildings are organized in a very formal layout; but a plan that has many qualities as has been proved decade after decade. Inside this plan, we have to define a space that is different from the existing space since the buildings on the campus are for either teaching or student housing – the undergraduates live on campus.

We are being asked to build a building that will be a meeting place, a sort of axis; a student centre of some twenty-five thousand square metres, with an auditorium for 1100 people that can be combined with a cinema seating 400, a radio station, a television studio, a large bookshop, restaurant spaces and a cafeteria; and also an electronic games room, and 6,000 letter boxes – because in an age when everyone is linked to a computer, we still need letter-boxes and a postman to deliver letters. And this incongruous mixture has to be integrated into the extraordinary constraints of what is more or less a historic site.

The project itself responds to the programme but seeks out the in-between, the moment where the programme has not been determined, i.e. movement, trajectories of users of the building – without going into detail, a strategic gap that will become the common denominator of the project.

One particularity of the site is that the Broadway side is half a storey lower than the campus side. We profited from this difference between the two wings of the building to create a system of ramps that not only make the project functional but also add a whole series of 'residual' spaces resembling airport lounges – places where people can wait, drink their coffee, play chess, consult their laptops. All this is located on the staircases and ramps which also provide space on two floors for the 6000 letter-boxes a setting for many activities.

The exterior, on one side, is at the traditional limit for a very simple reason: we are completing the nineteenth-century urban plan of McKim, Mead and White. This will, in fact, be our first contextual project.

On the other side, the part that opens onto the campus consists of a sort of screen of Chinese shadows with the ramps partly in translucent glass that lets through the light but also camouflages the places where chess is played, exhibitions are held, and televisions are located.

There are two other projects that I should like to mention in connection with the concept of programme-movement to attempt to show that it is the programme that generates the concept but that it is always necessary to find the gap, the space that has not been programmed.

First, the School of Architecture in Marne-la-Vallée. An architecture school is a challenge, at least for me because I spend a large part of my life running a school of architecture at Columbia. I had the impression that I knew too much about it. But I also found it very difficult because I said to myself: once the project is finished, we shall be criticized by the architecture students.

And so it was very worrying but as we did not expect to win we were very relaxed about it, which allowed us to design what we wanted to. This consisted of making a certain number of educational hypotheses: a certain number of non-hierarchized spaces – they were not studios with a specific mandarin, but all formed part of an activity space. Today, what is most lacking in architecture is not ideology but dialogue, polemics. And that is why we proposed that the school be organized around a space designed for meetings, circulation and movement: a public place that would also house exhibitions, juries, a cafeteria, amphitheatres and the library, which is always an important place in a school.

And so we have a setting around which the very precise part of the programme is organized, i.e. studios and lecture rooms. We sought to avoid any segregation between studios and lecture rooms as well as between administration and research buildings and lecture rooms; and so we distributed them throughout the whole periphery of this large interior space of about 25m by 100m.

There is one very important element that concerns us because it will have a marked effect on the life of the school. It has to be built in two stages: the first for 500 students, the second for 700; the passage from one stage to the next obviously presents difficulties, especially with regard to accessibility; and the budget is limited and therefore presents a challenge in the sense that it determined a certain number of our building choices.

On the exterior all the studios face north but they have glass windows onto the central space. This space thus becomes a great hall, which is not in the programme, inside a whole series of very precise, even banal responses to a fixed programme. As in the Columbia project, where the circulation spaces have become a place of animation, this gap is of the utmost importance.

The same approach applies to La Villette, despite its totally different context. At the Parc de la Villette, the way in which the circulation vectors intersect with the spaces marked by the *folies* seems to me symptomatic of our approach. The

> What is most lacking in architecture is not ideology but dialogue, polemics

architecture of the *folies* is not a formal composition, it is above all the result of where they are placed on the grid and the fact that the collision between the system of lines and system of points implies that certain elements of the *folies* become unrealizable, resulting in their absence. Consequently, part of the *folie* is expressed by the conveyer of movement. The architecture becomes heterogeneous, unfinished. It is not a question of a finished or an unfinished object; it is an object constantly in a state of becoming that is determined by the trajectories of movement. One piece of the *folie* disappears to leave room for the footbridge to the east-west gallery along the canal. Elsewhere a *folie* is intersected by the winding walk through the gardens that we have called the 'cinematic promenade' because it passes from one garden to another in an unexpected, almost sensual, mysterious way before passing through the folly halfway up and then the canal.

> When we look at La Villette at night...it is no longer an object or a space but simply a concept

And it is here, in this place of exception – it is no longer a garden – that we carry out our research. What applied to Groningen, where at the concept stage we tried to invent a building system, and to the Très Grande Bibliothèque – the running track also represents this place of invention – is also true here: we are trying to push the concept to its limits, sometimes to the absurd, to determine the whole architectural structure and detail. When we look at La Villette at night, there is this other possible reading of the park, when it is no longer an object or a space but, in its state of dematerialization, simply a concept.

This article is based on a lecture given by Bernard Tschumi in Paris. Translated from the French.

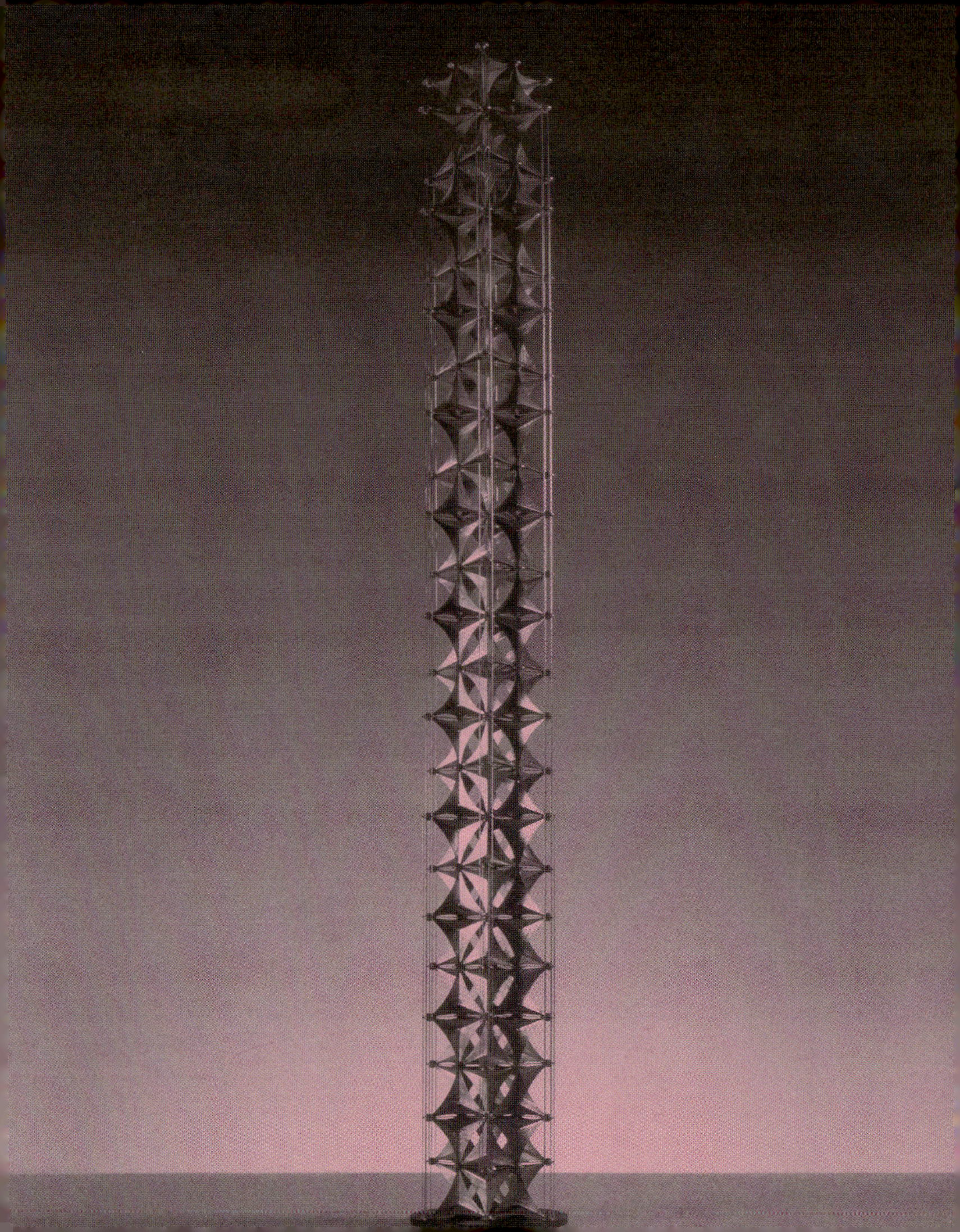

◀ EXPO 1970 Toshiba IHI Pavilion Tower. Photo: Tomio Ohashi

KISHO KUROKAWA

Abstract Geometry and Contemporary Architecture

In Japanese art, the greatest energy is poured into the invisible spaces between objects in order to determine their position. In other words, it is not the objects but their relationships that are the source of meaning

New Architecture 1: *Reaching for the Future*, 1997

If there is to be a new architectural style for the twenty-first century, it will probably be abstract symbolism. In the 1960s I predicted that as we approached the millennium, architecture would undergo a paradigm shift from the age of the machine principle to the age of the life principle. All of the concepts I discussed at that time – metabolism, metamorphosis, and symbiosis – are the most fundamental principles of life. Topos and interrelation are other important concepts that should be added to this group. Abstract symbolism is linked to this concept of interrelation and will be the key to a new horizon in architecture.

Abstract forms and geometrical figures have existed since ancient times. They were linked to the cosmologies of the different cultures in which they appeared. Each age has given different meanings to these geometrical figures or abstract forms. The abstract forms and geometry produced by the modern architecture and art of the twentieth century, though inheriting the legacy of Platonic geometry, expressed the spirit of the twentieth century through industrial society's image of the machine. But is it possible to create a new meaning by combining the abstraction of the twentieth century with the iconography of history, and the identity of topos with the cosmology of culture, yet another symbolic abstraction?

The task confronted by contemporary architecture (architecture after Modern Architecture) is how to escape binomial opposition and dualism and allow regionalism and internationalism, the past and the present, the identity of topos and universalism to exist in symbiosis.

The meaning we can obtain from abstract forms (geometric forms) is not a syntagmatic, linear thought process expressed as denotation but a paradigmatic, potential thought process expressed as connotation. Adorno, known for his philosophy of discontinuity, cites the example of Ulysses, saying that Joyce "by means of an analogy that links the present and the past, gives meaning, form and order to chaos."

In addition to giving ambivalent and polyvalent meaning to abstractions and geometrical forms through a double code, it is possible to give them the same meanings by introducing distortions and discontinuities into geometric forms with a twist that disrupts their symmetry or interrupts their rhythm. The curve of the wall in the Saitama Prefectural Museum of Modern Art and the curved wall of the atrium of the Nagoya City Art Museum represent such attempts.

What is common to all the new concepts of order that challenge Modernism is that the deconstructed parts are independent and at the same time create a dynamic, floating, and ever-changing order in which the part and the whole are in a mutually subsidiary relationship.

This type of creation of meaning through relationships can also be obtained by deconstructing one work of architecture, dividing it into its geometrical elements, and making them stand on their own before once again creating relationships.

In my museum at Louvain-la-Neuve, the conical forum rectangular exhibition wing, semi-circular lecture hall, and semi-circular amphitheatre are each independent, but are placed like the stepping stones in a Japanese garden, in random, free relationships. In Japanese art, the greatest energy is always poured into the invisible spaces between objects in order to determine their position. In other words, it is not the objects themselves but their relationships that are the source of meaning.

There are many examples of this: the stone garden at Ryoanji, the game of Go, calligraphy, and Zeami's *senuhima*, or moment of stillness, the silent interval in Japanese music called *Ma*. All of these are reflections of the Japanese aesthetic of asymmetry. We can call this the art of relationships.

The symbolism that manifests itself in topos, regionalism, and distinct cultures and traditions will be a key concept in the new intercultural age of the twenty-first century.

Two major approaches can be defined. One is to use abstract geometrical forms and manipulate, alter, and stagger their relationships to create completely novel meanings and narratives. For example, how is the axis of the building set? Is it symmetrical, does it establish the centre, is it complete, has another element (scenery, natural setting, an aperture, light, shadow, wind play) been incorporated between it and an opposing element? We know that an endless number of games, each unique, can be played simply by altering the placement (relationship) of the black stones and white stones used in the game of Go. We also know that great works of literature are composed of the ordinary, commonly understood words in the dictionary; again, it is the selection and arrangement of the words that make for great literature. The equivalent in architecture is to employ such geometrical abstractions as the helix, the cone, the cylinder, the four-sided and three-sided pyramid, the square, the triangle, the circle, the oval, and the lattice to express topos, regionalism, and a view of the universe.

The second approach is to abstract historical symbols. This strives for the same goal but from the opposite direction. Following this method, architecture is created by the abstraction of symbolic forms, symbolic signs, and traditional symbols through the process of intellectual manipulation.

When we speak of historical symbols in the context of Japanese architecture, the first things that come to mind are temples such as Horyuji and Todaiji, shrines such as Ise Shrine and Izumo Shrine, castle architecture such as Himeji Castle, the Katsura Detached Palace, and *sukiya*-style architecture. In all such architecture, the roof forms, post and beam structure and proportions, roof support structures and interior details are extremely sophisticated symbols, but in addition the ingenious relations inherent in the whole also create a symbolism. Those relations, in the examples that we call masterpieces, have achieved absolute perfection so that it is impossible to modify any detail without spoiling the whole. In addition, each work as a whole is an expression of the spirit of its age – the social background, the technological expertise – and the ideas and personality of its creator or creators.

The preservation of historic architecture is important precisely because the buildings are witness to the spirit of the age in which they were built. For us, who live in a different age, the challenge is whether we in turn can create architecture that will speak to future generations, an architecture that expresses the spirit of our age, our philosophy, our level of technological achievement, and our social context.

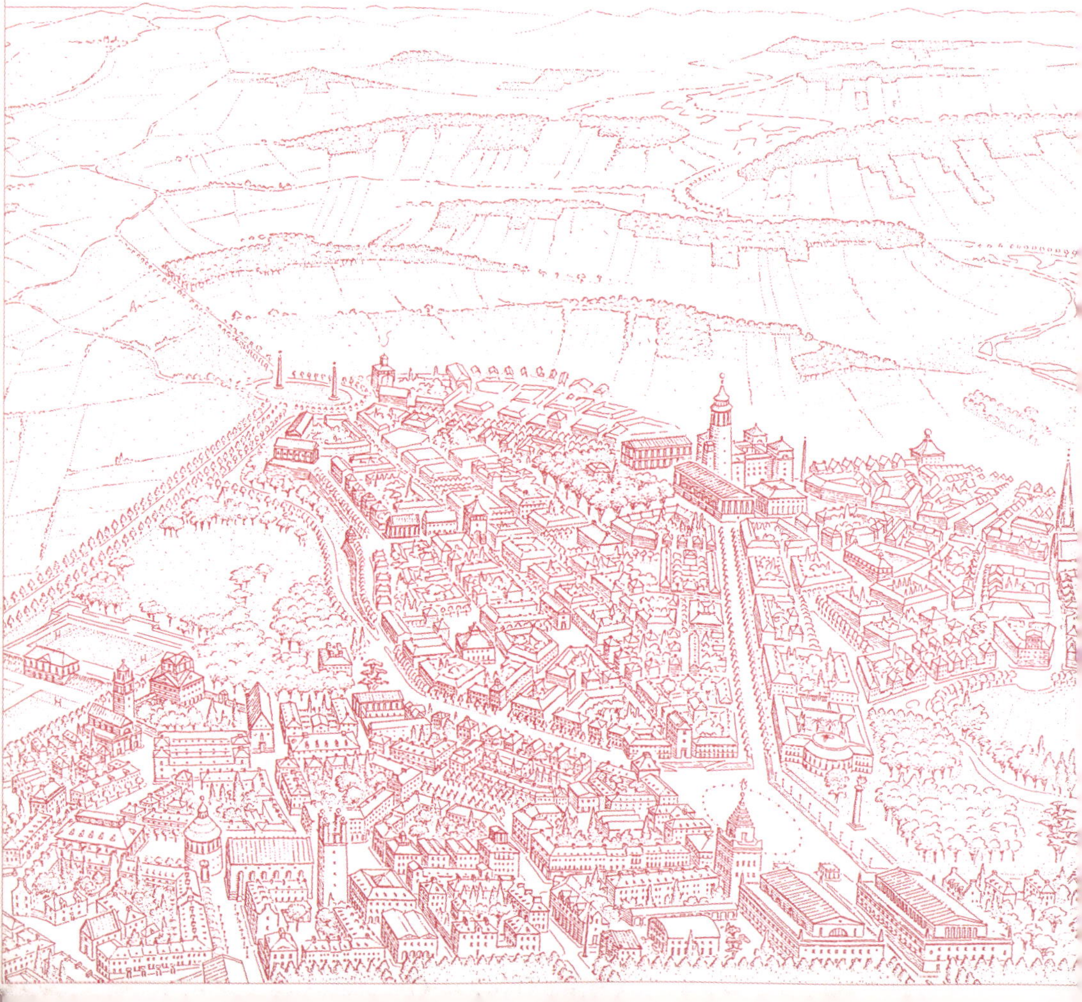

◀ The new town of Poundbury, Dorchester, Dorset, 1989. The town is composed of four independent quarters, each integrating all urbn uses within five minutes' walking distance

LEON KRIER

Prospects for a New Urbanism

A town is not the necessary, inevitable conclusion of the activities of a society. It is not an accident; it is a human invention

FORMS OF URBAN OVER EXPANSION

Most of the problems of our agglomerations have one basic cause: instead of growing organically by way of the multiplication of autonomous neighbourhoods, the cities of the twentieth century suffer from various forms of monofunctional overexpansion. This phenomenon creates disorder in their organization, in their functioning and in their appearance. It also generates dangerous imbalances between the centre and the periphery.

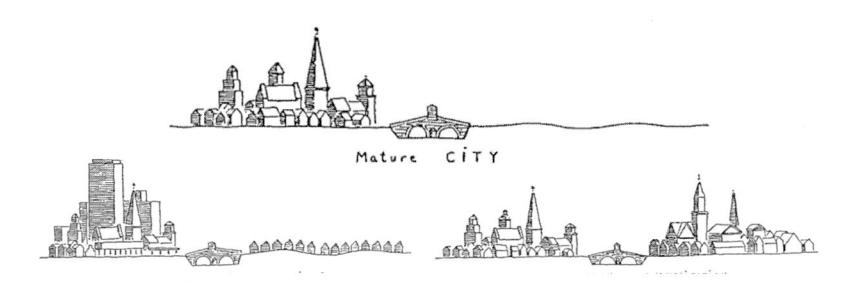

Mature City

THE NEED TO LINK ECOLOGY AND TOWN PLANNING

Any protest against the erosion of natural resources, or the destruction of our cities and countryside, remains futile if no reference is made to credible, workable solutions.

Local protest movements always get lost in details of larger-scale requirements for change motivated and guided by national and continental political decisions. Indeed, criticism without a plan often indicates an abdication of intelligence; for it demonstrates a fragmented view for which the city is the effect and the cause, the expression and the instrument.

Only a philosophical, technical, cultural, moral, economic, aesthetic plan on a global level can change the quality and aims of the imperatives for change in our natural and cultural environment. A coherent ecological plan is necessary to redefine the role, the authority and the legitimacy of architecture and urbanism.

The vertical overexpansion of city centres results in too many buildings, activities and users leading to excessive increases in the price of land and housing.

The horizontal overexpansion of the suburban peripheries resulting from the reasonable price of land, leads to areas of low density buildings and activities.

These two forms of excessive development feed each other. The functional problems that result are interdependent and cannot be resolved separately.

Cities and the countryside are a living reflection of our spiritual and material values. They express them and form them. They determine the way in which we use and squander our energy, time and land resources. The realization that we must perceive urbanism, agriculture and industry in ecological terms is the most urgent task and the one that poses the greatest challenge to industrial civilization. For the past two centuries technical advances have disrupted and undermined the customs and structures of society. The ecological ethics now being put in place are profoundly changing industrial technology and imperatives.

Today, a great deal of energy and imagination is devoted to producing so-called "ecological" buildings, tools and consumer goods. But such enterprises, although often praiseworthy, distract the general attention from the main aim of ecology, which must be contextual.

In the long term whether the air is polluted by public buses or private cars has little importance; the fact that the suburbanites live in houses that are ecologically perfect has no place in ecology.

The ecological challenge lies in the territorial reorganization of daily life within society. We are mistaken when we grant the name of town to any old cluster of buildings, for only in developed form can it merit that name.

A town is not the necessary, inevitable conclusion of the activities of a society. It can only be built and prosper if it fulfils the desires of individuals, of society and its institutions. It is not an accident; it is a human invention.

As such, it must first of all be the subject of a plan to make it a town. Manufacturing and commercial logic does not create towns that have any lasting quality, or any foundation for an enduring civilized society. Such necessary attributes as civic vitality, urban life, the beauty of a site, its identification as home, its landmarks, the pride of belonging to a neighbourhood, all spring from a vision of the city and its architecture.

Industry acts according to its own logic and occupies land in almost military fashion, causing maximum collateral damage. For this reason, an "ecological" plan cannot be limited to a city, a region or even a country. It must be examined in a continental context and be based on a charter for the environment and for the city. Such a charter should put forward typical solutions to typical

CITY & PARASITE

CITY without SUBURB

CITY with SUBURB

SUBURB without CITY

CITIES within the CITY

problems found on every scale in the city, the suburbs and the countryside.

Based on certainties proved by age-old practices, this charter must override partisan interests of political, industrial, financial and military authorities, local and national, religious and cultural groups. It must be based on a long-term political, cultural and economic consensus; it is the necessary complement of the political constitution of a modern nation, an ethical and civilizing plan of universal stature.

Berlin Tegel, an existing suburb consisting of urban fragments

Berlin Tegel, Krier urbanization project. Division of Tegel into four quarters, each with its own morphological and typological order

THE URBANIZATION OF SUBURBS

The metabolism between the suburbs and the centre is, from the outset, doomed to fatal corrosion; this fate must be reversed to avoid falling into barbarity. The enforced mobility of the suburban masses represents a threat to both cities and the countryside. This modern syndrome can only be checked by the creation of an urban civilization in the suburbs. The urban economy will no longer grow by expanding into the surrounding countryside, but by the development, the opening up, the completion, the internal growth of the suburbs. This must be the goal of a civilization that is truly "ecological." The transformation of the suburbs must occur through the abandon of functional zoning practices, by the redefinition and by the recomposition of density plans and of urban development programmes.

The polycentric reorganization of towns, that is to say the transformation of underdeveloped suburbs into autonomous, urban neighbourhoods will be the impetus for a process of territorial transformation, internal growth and the development of the suburbs.

It will make available for redevelopment vast tracts of housing estates, blocks of flats, single function business, educational, commercial, cultural, industrial centres, docks and disused industrial areas. Ecological development plans will bring to these specific urban areas the functions they are lacking and which are necessary for community life and for their autonomy.

The reorganization and reconstruction of badly organized zones will relieve the property pressure on the open country and in historic centres which, by definition, have reached an optimum degree of development with respect to density, forms and functions.

Today historic centres are the only true centres of city and civilized society. They account for only a tiny area in comparison with the vast stretches of suburbs.

Development tasks in historic centres should be redefined according to the following goals: to round off their perimeters and fill in fragmented areas by establishing street networks, building types, building techniques, an architecture in harmony with the site thus created; to remove single use, commercial, business and other colossi; to redevelop damaged zones by creating open spaces and traditional lots; to adjust the population density for the best functioning of the neighbourhood; to reintroduce the complete range of urban functions within walking distance.

All maintenance, conservation, restoration and rebuilding must be done using traditional techniques.

THE NEED TO REFORM DEVELOPMENT PROGRAMMES

The majority of the so-called "development programmes," such as housing estates, shopping centres, business parks are not defined by an urban philosophy but by developers, manufacturers, financiers and managers.

They are invariably horizontal or vertical over-concentrations of a single use in an urban zone, sometimes even in a single building or under a single roof.

The symbolic lack of quality of the majority of present building is the result of the functional monotony thus programmed and is the expression of it.

Density, function, location and, to a large extent, the form of these developments are decided before they drop on the architect's drawing board. Many architects are well aware that these programmes prevent them from designing true cities and villages but, individually, they are powerless to change the programmes without risking the loss of their commissions.

And so uniformity of use forces on even the best architects a choice that is limited to either a sincere but cruel expression of uniformity or variety that is always artificial because it has no basis in use. The results are inevitably without quality or they are kitsch, abstraction or caricature.

The symbolic wealth of urban architecture is based on the proximity of and dialogue between the greatest possible variety of private and public use, i.e. on the creation of open spaces, the urban fabric and the skyline of the city.

If we want the building sites of the future to contribute to an improvement in cities, villages and the countryside instead of adding to the disorder, new development programmes must consist of measures and elements that will fill the gaps in the suburbs and turn them into true city neighbourhoods.

THE MASTERPLAN, A DEFINITION

The plan, the skyline and the architecture of a city neighbourhood are determined by the masterplan. This is more than an architectural project, it is the prior condition for the integration of innumerable architectural projects in a coherent urban complex, the instrument that is necessary to create the harmony of the whole. It is much more than a technical tool: too many technically perfect masterplans during the post-war years led to the opposite. An excess of arbitrary regulations leads to tyranny and then to rejection. An excess of sophistication leads to innumerable possible deviations. It is above all the philosophy, the aims of a masterplan that count; those that lack them lead to exemplary monumental errors.

In the United States, the Loop, Chicago's business district, permits a built density that is the equivalent of the totality of office space for the whole country. In Italy, which has a total population of 57 million, all the city plans put together would allow for 180 million Italians to be housed in medium or low density developments. Again, in the United States, in 1935 the density of the total built area granted for the city of New York was sufficient to house the population of the whole world.

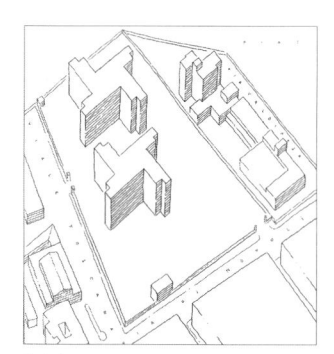

Existing state

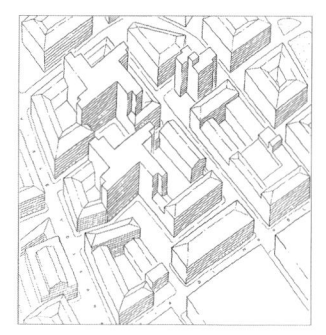

Krier plan

The masterplan is to the construction of a city what the constitution is to the life of a nation. It is much more than a specialized technical instrument and must be guided by an ethical and artistic vision. The masterplan represents the legislative form of such a vision; it is the geometric expression and the necessary complement of the law. To guarantee a concrete and sensitive homogeneity, it must have simple precepts. It is divided into five parts:

1. A plan of the city, defining the size and form of its neighbourhoods, parks and gardens.

2. A plan of the neighbourhood, defining the network of streets, squares and blocks.

3. The size of the lots on each urban block; number, shape and function of floors that can be built by lot.

4. The architectural code describing materials, technical configurations, proportions for external building elements (walls, roofs, windows, doors, porticoes and porches, garden walls, chimneys) and all built elements that are visible from public spaces.

5. A code for public spaces, defining the materials, groupings, techniques, design for paving and street furniture, road signs, other signs, lighting and planting.

The extraordinary geographical situation of the city of Luxembourg, forming an archipelago of quarters separated by deep valleys and gorges, constitutes a de facto demonstration of the theory of cities within the city

View of the new European quarters, Kirchberg, Luxembourg

The aim of the codes is to improve the quality of normal regular, inevitable building to create a "conventional" architecture of quality, to encourage the routine realization of commercial buildings by imitating long-established traditional building types, to reserve architectural expression and artistic rhetoric for the construction of public buildings.

Thus, the masterplan will ensure not only the harmonizing of often divergent interests but also the expression of the natural difference between private and public architecture. It is this dialectic, which gives profound character to a place, that will, one day, be worthy of the name "historic centre."

THE MASTERPLAN, A TOOL IN THE PUBLIC INTEREST

In Europe, public authorities have for a decade now almost completely abandoned their role as clients in the fields of architecture and urban planning; even in France, the *grands projets* are limited to prestige projects.

New division into quarters. Maximum size of a quarter is 33 hectares with 10,000 inhabitants

If it is the market economy that now determines the shape of our environment, we should ask ourselves first of all whether it is capable of creating public spaces. In fact, it may well be that the majority of buildings put up by a market economy will, in the future, be a succession of private enclosed spaces with limited public access such as shopping centres, schools, condominiums, housing estates and traffic infrastructure (motorways, stations, airports). Secondly, can public spaces such as streets, squares, parks (a major public asset) that have accrued for centuries until, for Europeans, they have become second nature, survive in a market economy that is not primarily motivated by the general interest but by private investment and profit?

In every country, it appears that developers, private bodies and institutions, however well intentioned, are not able to build and preserve public spaces that are in any way the equal of European historic centres. Although commerce is a constituent part of public space, it does not justify it on its own. The establishment and maintenance of a true public space is first of all a matter of general interest, of citizenship, of community construction. In the United States, the creation of public space has been left to the private sector; federal revenues that should be used to create public spaces have been diverted from this civilizing role and are used to repair the damage caused by unrestrained capitalism.

In totalitarian regimes, on the other hand, the expansion of the public sector to the detriment of the private sector has led to a dilution of even the concept of public space.

What private developers are interested in is the commercial aspect of public space. They are, therefore, unsuitable as legislators or creators of masterplans for large urban areas. And yet this is the modus operandi that is the norm in all developed countries. The correct, balanced mix of urban functions is a constitutional matter. When architects work for important private developers they are subject to private interests; while they are dependent, they are not asked to write masterplans. Technically speaking, and in the true sense of the term, an architect who is the author of a masterplan should have the independence of a legislator, and his loyalty should be to the public interest rather than the private interests of shareholders.

If market forces, on the one hand, and the machinery of the State, on the other, have both proved incapable of creating true public space, we should conclude that it is for public authorities to produce masterplans as legislative instruments expressing in three dimensions (in plan and in section) a synthesis of public and private interests. This is indispensable for the fate of our cities.

From Léon Krier: *Architecture: Choice or Fate?*, Papadakis Publisher, London, 1997

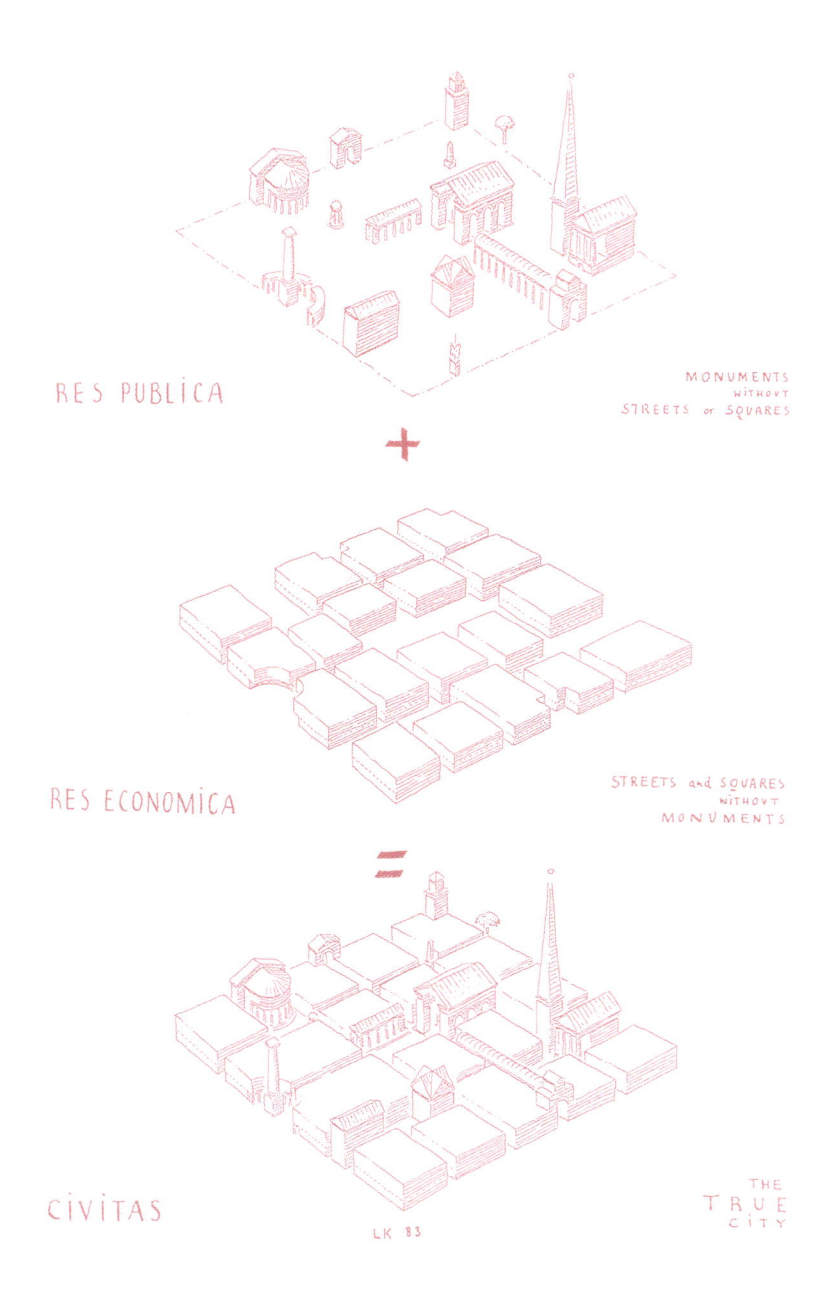

RES PUBLICA — MONUMENTS WITHOUT STREETS or SQUARES

+

RES ECONOMICA — STREETS and SQUARES WITHOUT MONUMENTS

=

CIVITAS — THE TRUE CITY

LK 83

COOP HIMMELB(L)AU

The Architecture of Clouds

Coop Himmelb(l)au is not a colour but an idea – the idea of having architecture with fantasy, as buoyant and variable as clouds

Coop Himmelb(l)au, 1968

The city is like a field of clouds. The rubber grid of a networked city. The builders of the Tower of Babel were missing the material reinforced concrete. We are missing the material of the confusion of languages which we need to complete it.

There is no solution for the city. The strategies of urban planning operate on the matrix of diverging impossibilities. The architect has to choose one and claim responsibility for it.

Clouds are symbols for conditions that change quickly. They form and transform themselves through the complex interaction of changing situations. Viewed in slow motion, the architecture of urban development could be compared with patches of cloud.

The vocabulary of urban planning should be in an architectural antique shop and replaced by phantasms still to be defined, which fluctuate and flicker like a television screen after a broadcast. The white noise of urban strategy, as a digitally networked system without hierarchy, is the play of suburb and periphery, which will mould and determine the image of our cities and the quality they have to offer.

The notions of centre, axis and spatial sequence will have to be replaced by tangent, vector and sequence of images. We should not regret the loss of public space, but reinterpret it as a fluctuating, networked mediated event. One that behaves more like a semi-conductor than a sequence of spaces.

The development of architecture is also furthered by strategies that are compromised by searching for lines and fields of possibilities tied together by chance, anti-logic and anti-authority. But the coincidence of systems – both as built space and as media space – becomes the basis for new designs and projects, the rubber grid as the premonition of a dynamic design-net for cities like clouds.

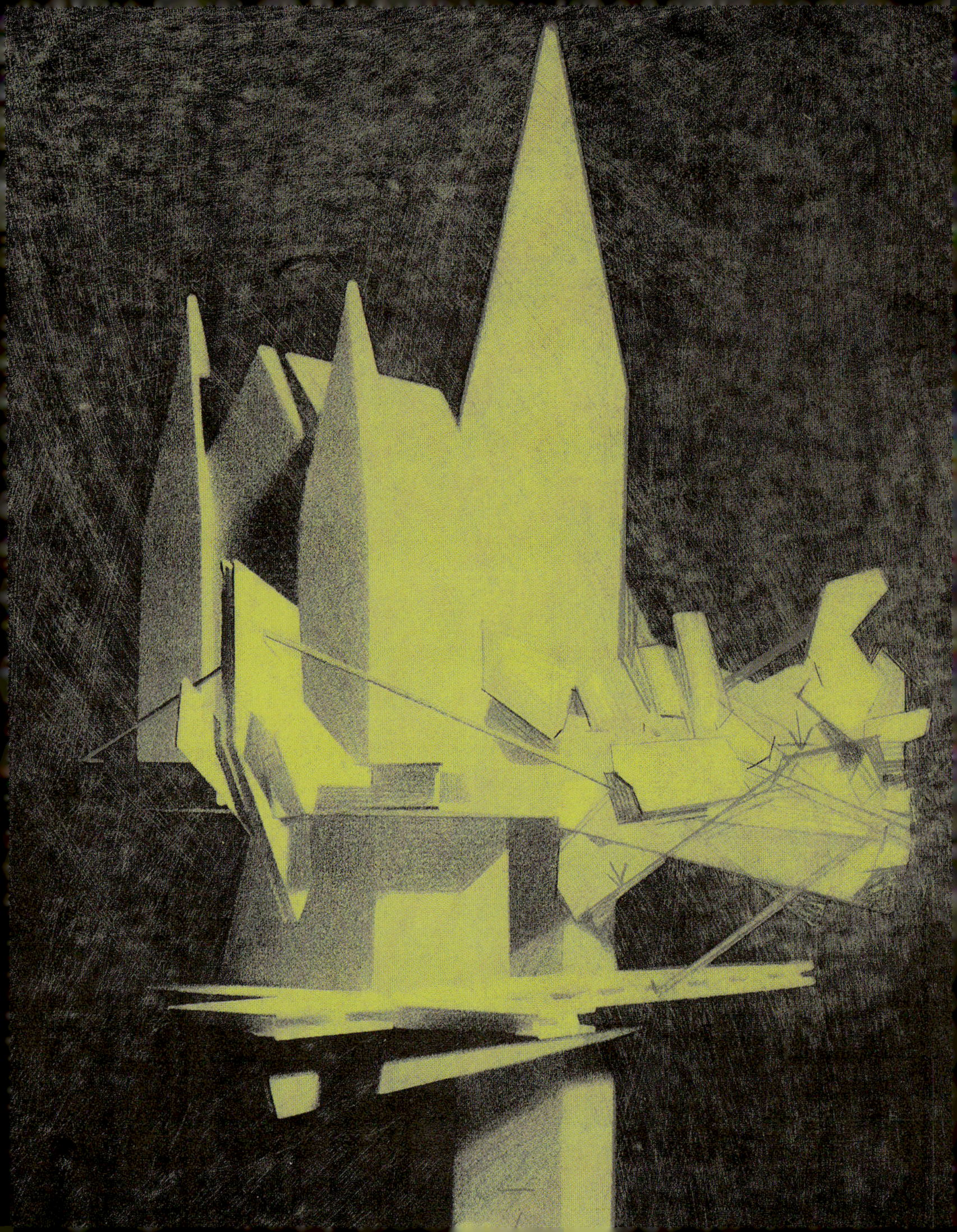

◀ Siteline Vienna: Conceptual study Stefansdom

LEBBEUS WOODS

The Crisis of Innovation

This is the way the world ends,
This is the way the world ends,
Not with a bang, But with a whimper

T.S. Eliot, *The Hollow Men*, 1925

It is not entirely clear to me why Andreas Papadakis has taken up "the end of innovation" as a prospect architects should, at the end of the century and the millennium, consider. But I am glad he has. By raising the issue he calls into question an idea too long taken for granted and long overdue for criticism. I am not referring only to the idea of innovation-as-progress contained within post-modernist critiques of modernism, which are not only highly competitive, thus antagonistic from the start, but also too quick to consign innovation to a historical scheme that deprives it of any possible poetic vitality today. What is needed instead is a fresh look at innovation as a force that may still serve humanist, if not modernist, ends in spite of all post-modernist disdain for both.

For thoughtful observers today, innovation has a host of negative aspects. It is first of all associated with exploitation, chiefly because of the manipulation of ever-changing fashions and trends, which yields celebrity and notoriety for a few clever self-promoters, and always translates into someone's financial gain.

What is needed is a fresh look at innovation as a force that may still serve humanist, if not modernist, ends in spite of all post-modernist disdain for both

Or, the exploitation of the global marketplace by the mass-marketing of new products, "new" meaning everything from new-everywhere to new-only-there, in the "developing markets" of Eastern Europe, Asia, Africa, South America, which are desperate for signs of "first world" status, however regressive, outdated, or banal these may be.

Another negative for innovation is its continuing alliance with big business, the multi-national corporate structure whose financial machinations continue as they have throughout the last two centuries to run roughshod over political, ecological, and cultural landscapes in pursuit of their own interests. Few would disagree today that the various national governments are not to some considerable extent surrogates of the most powerful international corporations, and have to the same degree become identified by and with their interests, often at the expense of concerns for which they are the supposed stewards. The battle over the European Union, to cite only the most current example, centres on the issue of a common European currency and related economic matters — social and cultural issues are entirely subsumed in financial ones. Innovation, in this and similar schemata — like the controversial GATT treaty in the United States — is only the measure of a market "edge" that determines big winners and losers in the games of global capital.

But the most damning aspect of innovation comes from its tricky relationship with the idea of progress. "Progress," Herbert Marcuse wrote, "becomes quantitative and tends to *delay indefinitely the turn from quantity to quality* [author's italics] — that is, the emergence of new modes of existence with new modes of reason and freedom." Quantity is mathematically certain, the main ingredient of the "bottom line" profit margin of corporate enterprise, whereas quality is negotiable, manageable, manipulable, a kind of phantom that has no specific place in ledgers, but is nonetheless subject to them.

However, many promises made at the beginning of the last century — the century of modernization — were qualitative and foretold of broad human progress that would result from discoveries of science and technology, applied through art and design. Many of the quantitative promises were kept: bigger, faster, more complex have certainly been achieved in modern societies. But they have often been achieved at the cost of concepts such as social justice and universal human suffrage that have also been promised, a reward to the great masses of industrial workers who have actually built modern technological society. Even worse, the effects of global and regional wars, of ecological disasters, of rising unemployment and declining environmental quality in many cities, of diminishing purchasing power of most wage earners, of reduced health care and educational opportunities, and other erosions of the quality of life for many, have given rise to political and cultural reaction, which threatens the hard-won gains of modern society. Resurgent nationalism and regional chauvinism are all that are left of the globalisation game. Progress for some has translated into regress for many.

Under the duress of fear or disillusion, it is extremely difficult for "new modes of existence with new modes of reason and freedom" to emerge. They, of course, cannot emerge of their own accord, but only as a result of conscious, and concerted, human action. In their place today much innovation is directed toward quantitative goals, managed by the corporate stewards of modernization, and results in the creation only of new modes of entertainment, distraction, and consumer passivity. *Circus et panem*, technocratic style.[1]

Art and design, and architecture in particular because it unifies them, have been a significant part of both the promise and failure of modernization, at least in qualitative terms. There has been plenty of innovation by architects, from the beginning of the last century to the present but it has had less and less to do with improving the general quality of human existence, as the decline of the most innovative architects' interest in housing clearly demonstrates. Today, following the general cultural trend, the greatest innovations are in museums, which, together with cinemas, theme park buildings, libraries, and concert halls, can arguably be considered, from the public's point of view, as places of high-end, up-scale entertainment, and in many cases themselves as a secondary source of entertainment, when experienced through television, magazines and books. The point here is not that these are unworthy cultural productions, but just the opposite:

that they represent perhaps all too well a society that has shifted its qualitative concerns from broad improvements in the human condition to narrow ones, a society in which, it is only fair to say, innovation has been subsumed almost entirely by the quantification not simply of culture, but of the human condition itself.

When the modern era was still innocent of itself, the work produced by the Bauhaus, the Suprematist and Constructivist, De StijI, Futurist, Expressionist, and other, independent architects[2] was vivid with a power to rally and coalesce industrial society's emerging energies into a new collective/urban world, one that relied without apology upon materialism and the idea of continuous innovation. What was needed, they argued, was a new architecture and urbanism, a new materiality and order of materiality that were required not to complete, nor, even less, to "express" *post facto* the processes of radical change, but to actively initiate them. Only when new types of space were constructed, offering the potential to be inhabited in new ways, could the ethics, politics and culture of modernity be defined, implemented, and realized. Even before modern social institutions were well defined, as in post-World War I Germany and Russia, architects brazenly assumed a leading role, becoming the vanguard of a better society they believed would surely come.

Pulsing beneath the architects' audacity was their faith in the capacity of people (inspired, perhaps, by their example) to create their own destinies, and the means by which to attain them. Sant'Elia's statement, "Each generation must build its own city," could not have been made without his conviction that each generation would want to be as innovative as he perceived his own to be, and that architecture could be the primary instrument of effecting social change. But as the century neared its end, it was very clear that neither has proved to be the case.

> Innovation has been subsumed almost entirely by the quantification not simply of culture, but of the human condition itself

The problematic inherent in optimistic projections about the relationship of architecture to social change and political power is that the most innovative architects chose to be sanguine, whereas the regimes they imagined themselves allied with, such as those of revolutionary Russia or post-war America, treated architects and architecture more as pawns than protagonists.

Eventually, architects became aware of the fact that the various institutions behind modernization were less interested in architectural expressions of social ideals than in tangible, quantitative results. After all, by the mid 1940s, the early, hairy days of the founding of socialist and capitalist societies, when innovative designs were useful as instruments of propaganda and persuasion (and rarely built), were over. What was needed then were large-scale works, more engineering than architecture, that fulfilled grand post-World War II economic schemes, which led eventually to "globalisation," and also special, symbolic buildings that reassured all concerned that culture was not being ground to dust under a new form of totalisation. The focus today on innovative buildings of this latter type speaks more than anything of architects' acceptance of the terms of this new stage of modernization harsher reality.

Each generation must build its own city
Sant'Elia

Where once the most innovative architects felt confident enough of their ethical footing to propose designs that took the lead in transforming existing ways of living, today's leading architects concern themselves primarily with recasting in new forms familiar and already established ideas of social life and experience. Confronted with the dramatic and sometimes tumultuous social changes now affecting cities, these architects demur, preferring instead to address in their work high-profile building types where innovation is confined to formal, not existential, aspects of design. Innovation has, as a result, become synonymous with fashion, sensation and celebrity, and no longer with the goal of initiating, and of leading, social change.

In reaction, the younger generation of architects today, idealistic as ever and therefore wishing to avoid the shallowness of being mere stylists, often consider the making of new types of forms anathema, a mark only of the hubris of architects. Far from being considered as a means of changing the human condition for the better, the invention of radically new forms and spaces seems to many socially irresponsible. Innovation, therefore, is justifiable only within the framework of the already known and accepted. Rem Koolhaas, whose ideas about architecture and urbanism are both revealing and influential, has claimed that in the early days of the last century, the heroic position was one of rebellion against convention, against the established norms of society. Today, however, the heroic position is one of going along with what he calls "the inevitable," of accepting and working within the mainstream.[3]

Implicit in this statement is a resigned assessment of the status and the state of contemporary architecture, both of which have fallen far in their impact on and relation with today's most pressing social, cultural and political conditions.

And it is difficult to argue, in practical terms, with this assessment. Looking back over the century, it is painfully obvious that all the bold social innovations initiated at its beginning, which architects sought to lead with their innovative designs, have failed, leaving in the end no socially cohering ideals for architects to codify in terms of urban space and form. Indeed, the boldest innovations of modern architecture itself – in mass housing and urban planning – failed to the same degree, and for the same reasons. Lacking any ideals of social progress to coalesce in great building projects, architects today do not have the confidence, the will or the desire to lead in the innovation "of new modes of existence with new modes of reason and freedom." Because they have convinced themselves that they only serve a society over which they have no control, and in which their authority is greatly diminished, they wait dutifully for orders from further up the economic chain of command. As Rem Koolhaas has also noted, "For their thoughts to be mobilized architects depend on the provocations of others – clients, individual or institutional."[4] Architects no longer feel responsible for initiating social change through their designs; nor for their own narrowing of scope within its dynamics; nor even for the end of innovation, as they might once have conceived it. They have returned this responsibility to the individuals and institutions who held it before the beginning of the century, before the advent of modernity, with its promises of empowering the great numbers of people through new social, political and cultural institutions. In this sense, innovation has indeed come to an end. Tragically, I would say, and almost completely.

My "almost" is of course the fragile thread on which my own work, indeed my very belief in architecture, precariously hangs. Whether the thread connecting architecture to the more universal human condition breaks in my case is merely a matter of personal concern. However, if it should break at the weak points it now exhibits for the present society generally, the results will be catastrophic, and probably irreversible.

I will close with a brief reflection that can be seen as a cross-section through this thread. "Whereof one cannot speak," said Ludwig Wittgenstein, "thereof one must remain silent." Surely he was thinking of the poetic. The poetic cannot really be spoken "about" but only in its own terms. The poetic has everything to do with knowledge. Let us say that it is a particular kind of knowledge. Like all knowledge, however, the poetic must be manifest in some tangible, perceptible way. Unlike most knowledge, however, this tangibility exists only in an absence, absence understood not as nothingness, but as the space of something that exists but is missing.

Arthur Schopenhauer said that beauty is the knowledge we gain from pleasure, whereas the sublime (which is closer to the "poetic" in our sense here) is the knowledge we gain from suffering. It is, in other words, a particularly important knowledge implicit in everything around us, but which can never be explicitly present. There is no doubt that we experience the knowledge of this crucial absence as a deep kind of suffering.

However, Jean-François Lyotard has said, "It is clear that it is not our business to supply reality but to invent allusions to the conceivable which cannot be presented." He chooses to face forthrightly the task at hand, "inventing allusions to the conceivable." The absent knowledge can be alluded to, if not presented. It can, in short, be realized through evocation.

The evocation of the absent, through allusion, suggestion, through the making felt as sharply as possible the absence itself, is the first and most important task of art.

What, then, is this knowledge of something which is implicit in everything around us and yet which cannot be presented, therefore is always missing? Let us say that it is *the knowledge of the whole*.

We experience the world only in fragments and yet, the unfolding of time, the experience of growth and decay, the many similarities between our experiences and those of others, and even the differences in these experiences imply an order inherent in all things and events. We sense this order most especially in the organic unity of our physiological and mental processes, in the very thoughts of 'a whole' to which all the fragments must, we believe, belong. These thoughts are the origin of our personal authenticity, and thus of our need to innovate, to invent our own existences out of the fragmentary substance of our experiences of the world.

> It is clear that it is not our business to supply reality but to invent allusions to the conceivable which cannot be presented
> — *Jean-François Lyotard*

It has been said that every artist creates a world. What this statement means is that every artist worthy of the name evokes a world, because a world, a whole, cannot be literally created, made present, without itself becoming a fragment.

Only the innovation inherent in a work of art evokes "the conceivable which cannot be presented." And innovation occurs only when the artist takes a special kind of risk. This is the risk of working and living in the paradoxical, in the intense materiality of what is present that creates in us an experience of what is not. It is the risk of understanding the potential of the human to be human, without ever fully realizing it. This is the risk of the poetic, and the very crisis of innovation.[5]

Notes:
[1] "Entertainment and Bread" were what Roman tyrants like Diocletian believed were sufficient to pacify the masses, and make them easy to rule.
[2] See author's article, "Utopia Unbound: Russian and Soviet Avant-Garde, 1915-32," A+U (Architecture and Urbanism), Tokyo, February 1993, pp. 4-11. A discussion of the relationship between art and power.
[3] Said in response to a question posed by the author, during a colloquium held at the Urban Center in midtown Manhattan, March, 1994
[4] Rem Koolhaas, *S, M, L, XL*, Monacelli Press, 1995, p. xix
[5] Written for the seminar course given by the author entitled "Ethics of the Poetic" with fifth year students at the Irwin S. Chanin School of Architecture of The Cooper Union, New York City, February, 1997

Siteline Vienna ▶

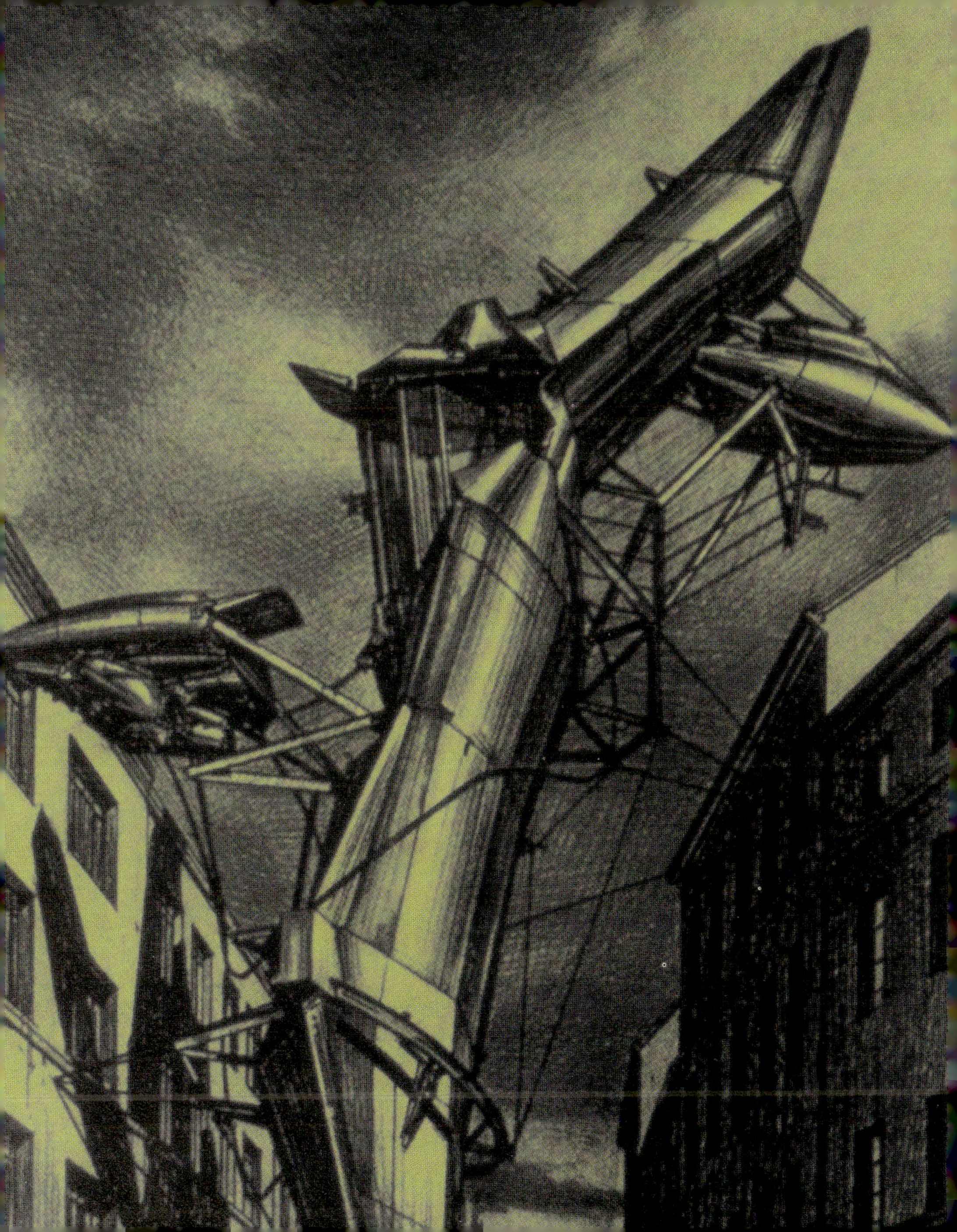

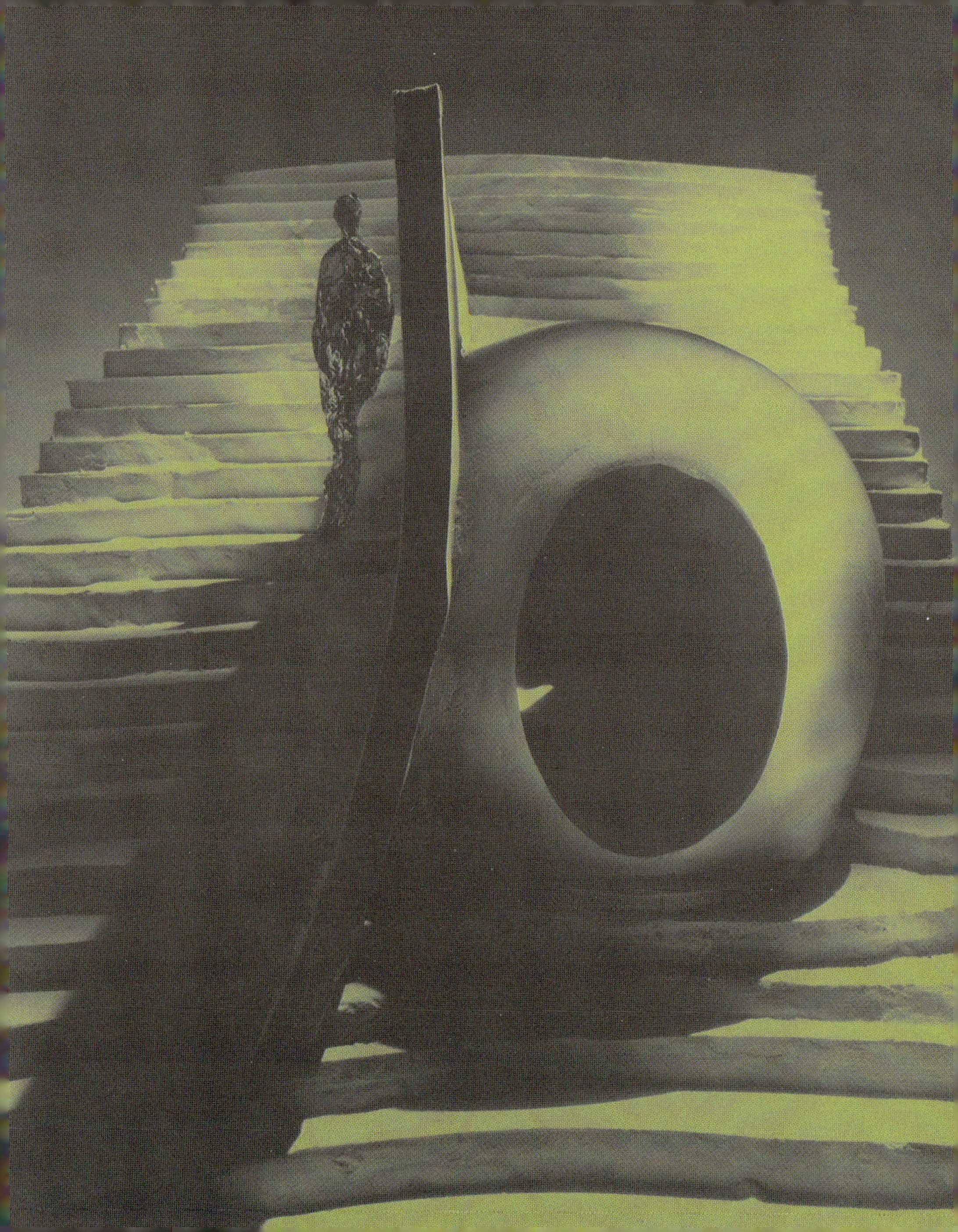

◀ Philip Johnson: The Wayfarers' Chapel

DIMITRI FATOUROS

The End of Place?

*Instead of creative coexistence between human beings,
what is on offer today is degeneration and forced isolation*

New Architecture 2: *The End of Innovation in Architecture*, 1998

If architecture is the art of the creation of place where does that leave the question of the end of architecture? If architecture is just an "object" indifferent to the human condition, asking only for the incorporation of effervescent impressions into urban scenarios or open-air landscapes then even when it pretends to represent place, if it is gigantic or not to scale it will always be both aggressive and cynical with respect to the poetic quality of the human habitat. But it is this kind of "object" that is offered by the main trends of architecture today, opening an era of monopolisation of the environment. They accept and absorb any transformation and any combination of technology and subordinate architecture to an exercise in media-technology and propositions for so-called new needs and uses. Their *uncritical* use pays no heed to how and where they are applied. Such "objects" transform promenades and sequences of body movement into transfer corridors and mass transportation links. The serenity of the protective cell and the shadows of glorious porticoes are transformed into calculated constructions that obey either facile mechanistic statistics or expressionistic graphics.

If architecture is the creation of *place* or *locus* or *topos*, meaning the creation of physical and symbolic situations for the understanding and contemplation of the human condition then the question takes on a different hue. In this case, the environment projected by these "objects," offers relationships that include creative interaction, respect for one another, sympathetic living space, the sensual attractiveness of shadows, and a sense of serenity and passion for the quietness of the cell, creating an environment ensuring a way of life that represents the creation of place.

It is interesting to note that the supporters of these "objects" with sarcastic cynicism define as minimal an expression of any creation of place that does not accept their "objects". And so the desire for a non-gigantic and "non-noisy" environment is considered only as a low profile expression of their work.

Instead of lively co-habitation with new everyday facilities that make full use of all that new technologies with their magical possibilities can add to the quality of life and to the quality of place, these facilities are used only for show and ostentation. Instead of creative coexistence between human beings, what is on offer today is degeneration and forced isolation. Isolated individuals perform as components of various super-competitive entities, instead of trying to cultivate togetherness and the qualities of the person.

If this is the case, at least in the more publicised trends of today's architecture, then the place that architecture should create is endangered, perhaps even lost.

Within this frame, despite the deterministic and futurological flavour of the question, we may objectively ask if this is the end of the *city* signifying the establishment of the mechanically assembled element of agglomerations and the accumulation of perishable and insecure individuals. In other words, the question is whether the members of the community of the city, the *citizens*, may be facing their end.

Following this line of thought, the discussion about the end of architecture may lead to questions concerning the heart of the existence of the human condition.

One way out of this situation may be to re-introduce *nature* into the man-made environment, not as a garden or landscaping technique, but as a way of life. In other words, to understand nature as a criterion for the relationship of man with the environment as expressed in the habitat. Architecture can thus create places where fascinating new technologies are introduced and where learn-ing from nature and coexisting with nature provide creative possibilities for human life. The question may then be defined as follows: whether or not this is the end of *architecture*, the existence or not of *architecture* is a question of the existence of *human* culture.

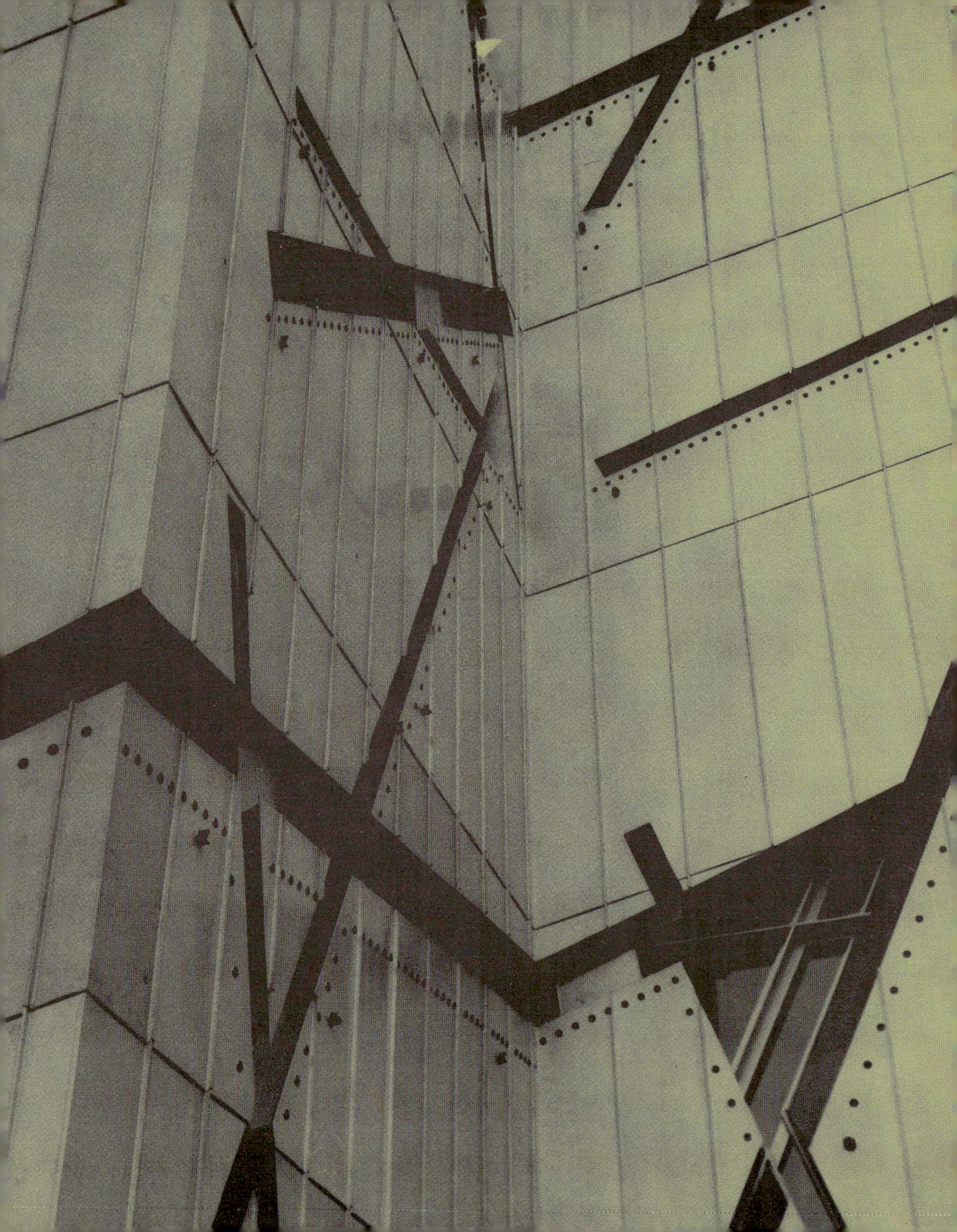

◀ The Jewish Museum, Berlin

DANIEL LIBESKIND

Traces of the Unborn

*The city is the greatest spiritual creation of humanity;
a collective work which develops the expression of
culture, society, and the individual in time and space*

New Architecture 2: *The End of Innovation in Architecture*, 1998

For some time now I have been working on a project I have termed the "Traces of the Unborn" – a term describing the need to resist the erasure of history, the need to respond to history, the need to open the future: that is, to delineate the invisible on the basis of the visible. Out of this meditation I have developed certain planning and architectural concepts which reflect my interest and commitment to the memory of the city; to the time in which it dwells; and to the freedom it represents.

Even if anywhere-becoming-somewhere arrives, the age of closure of sites might yet bid farewell to *genius loci*, that idol of politics, the ultimate onto-theological component of Architecture appropriated.

The consideration of these issues with respect to the future development of the contemporary city raises fundamental questions concerning damage to urban fabrics past, present and future, whether this damage is caused by war, economic conditions, or political ideology. Faced with these conditions, contemporary urbanism must leave aside conventional forms of contextualism and utopianism in favour of strategies enabling the transformation and metamorphosis of existing realities which take the discontinuity of the city as a positive point of departure for the construction of new urban perspectives.

The *genius loci* is but a realm invested with twenty centuries of metaphysical oppression masking the impotence of ecumenic empires to control places and the human addiction to the orientation of space.

There is an important need in every society to identify the icons which constitute a particular area, the structures which form the texture of living memory. In refuting the past and future alike, the eternal present of transformation and metamorphosis must be incorporated into an urban framework which encourages the creation of unpredictable, flexible and hybrid architectures. At the same time the given should not be treated as an obstacle or as a form of pathology, but rather as an opportunity pregnant with new relations and urban experiences.

The implications for the city and Architecture which follow from the de-theoretization of somewhere are constructively exhilarating.

It is necessary for contemporary architects and planners to challenge the whole notions of the Masterplan with its implied finality; its misguided ambition of eternal recurrence of the same through replication. Rather, they must develop open and ever changeable methodologies which reinforce the processes of transformation and articulate the dynamic of change in a diverse and pluralistic architecture. They must both trace and steer through time and space the course of the city; the city as both memory and a dream; as the House of Being and the Matrix of Hope.

The line of incision cutting the mind is straight and long – slice manipulating dearth.

Following Paul Valery's axiom that "humanity is permanently threatened by two dangers: order and disorder." My own search for a new and responsive urbanism navigates between the Scilla of nostalgic historicism and the Charybdis of totalitarian *tabular rash*. In doing so, it rejects both simulation in the service of respectful modesty, and destruction in the service of ideological purity. It is the search for a process which seeks to define the often invisible meanings embodied in the misunderstood, discarded, transient or forgotten topologies and situation which make up the scientific energy of the city. It addresses the city's complex history as a heterogeneous spatial and temporal network, whose connections and contradictions form the basis for critical modes of intervention.

Is there a site somewhere, which does not commemorate the 'turn' of history toward its own presence, while anticipating someone else's absence?

The resulting structures suggest a new connection or knot between urban areas and their surroundings, between buildings and their sites, interacting with existing conditions by both supplementing and subverting networks of traffic, street patter, building and open space. They are open, flexible matrices, out of which can emerge forms of architecture and urban space whose expression and representation are indistinguishable from the political space they occupy. This matrix presents a histogram of invisible realities and their relations, a graph in time and space describing the equation of a city's soul.

Is there a place anywhere – even somewhere out of this world – which does not claim to be the focal point for the transport of Being, a Being always disappearing in a post-mortem of the future?

The city is the greatest spiritual creation of humanity; a collective work which develops the expression of culture, society, and the individual in time and space. Its structure is intrinsically mysterious, developing more like a dream than a piece of equipment. Given this, alternatives are required to traditional urban planning ideas, which imply continuity based on projection. My own project in search of the contemporary city represents one possible alternative – an approach which understands and celebrates the city as an evolving, poetic and unpredictable event.

The Jewish Museum, Berlin ▶

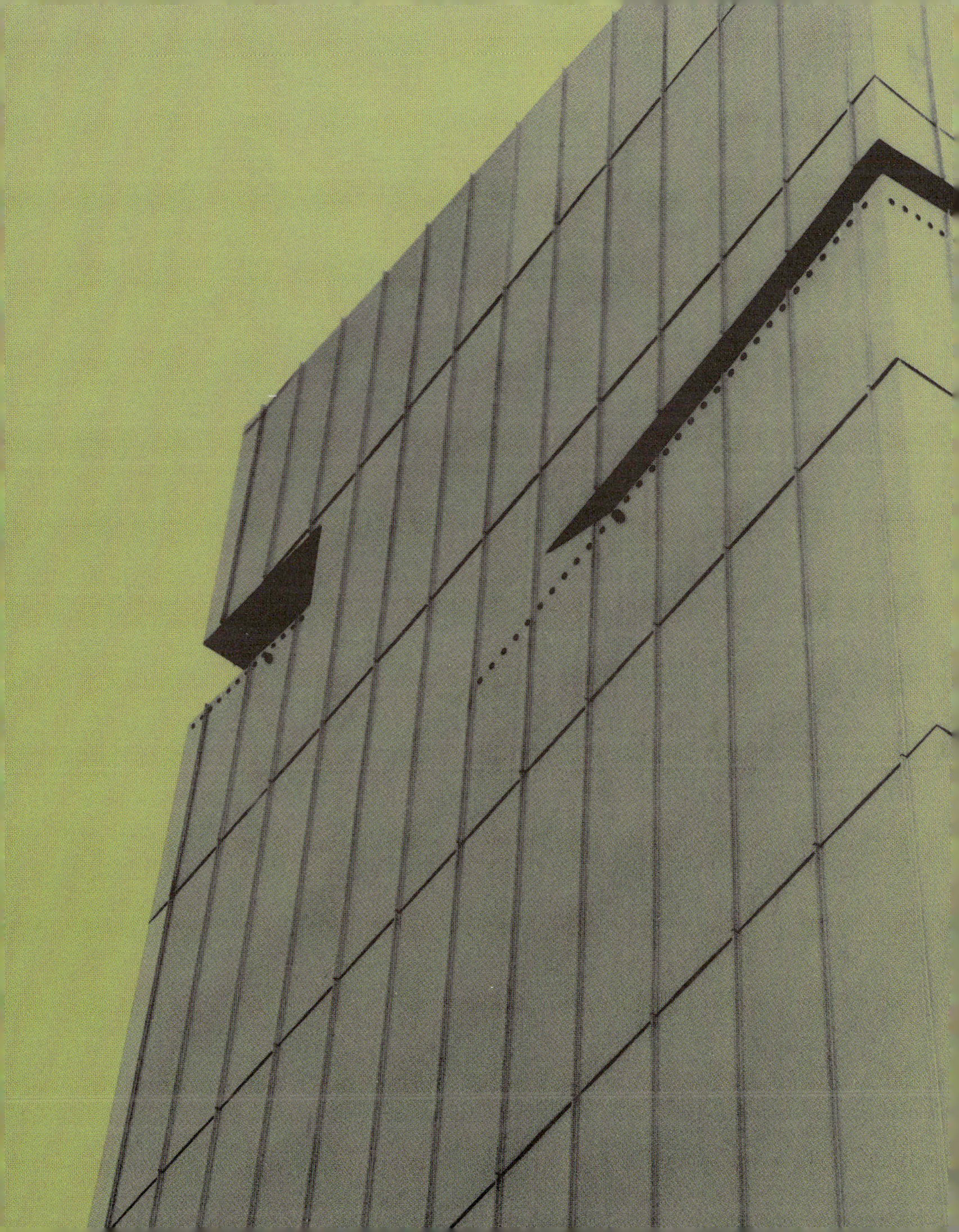

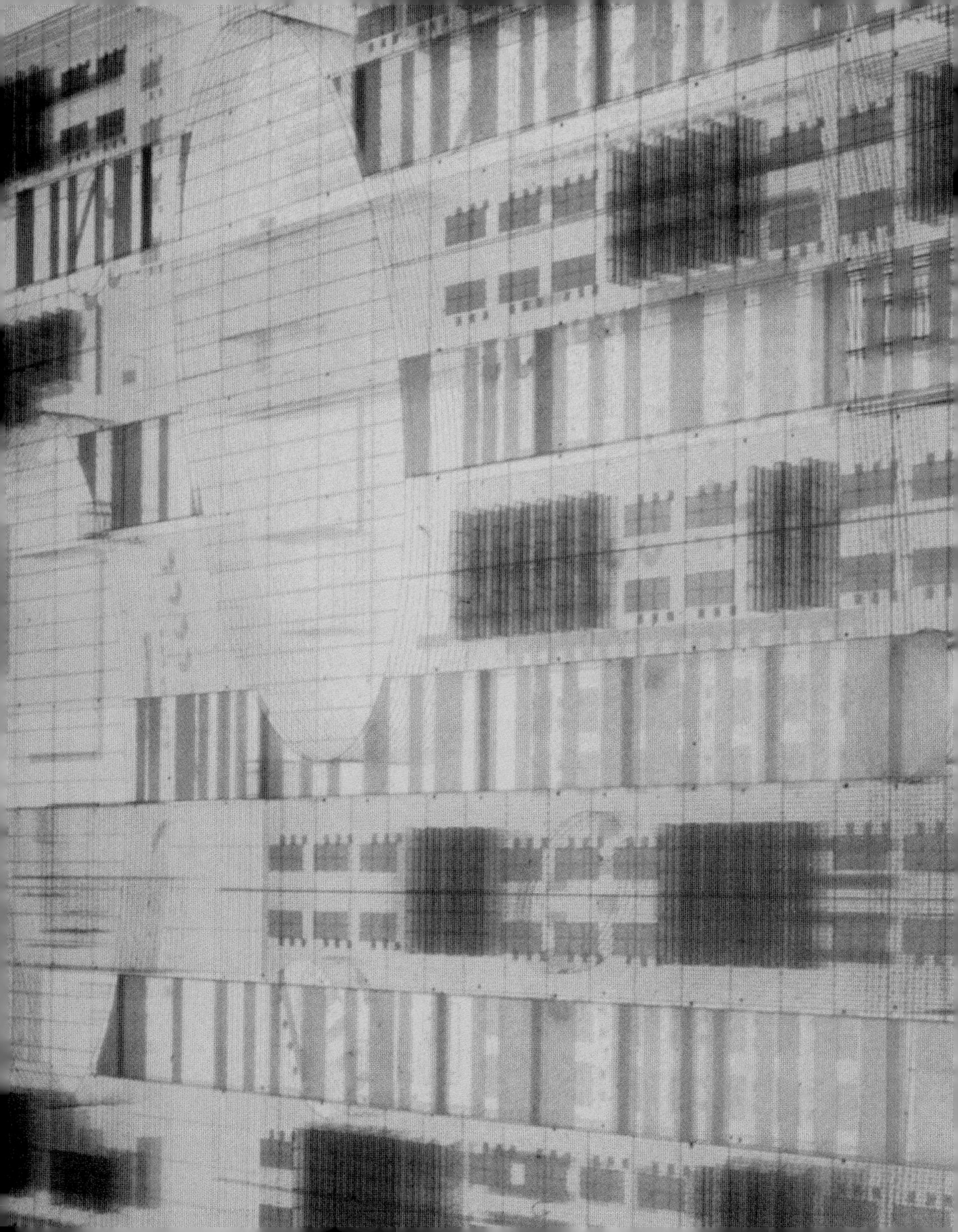

TOYO ITO

Three Transparencies

Despite our apparent transparency we continue to build ever more solid barriers between us. The key lies in introducing new openings through the walls we have already built

FLUID TRANSPARENCY

To stand before a giant fish tank at the aquarium is to experience the curious sensation of being in two places at once. With only a clear wall in between, "here" on this side one is on dry land surrounded by air, while "over there" on the other opens an aquatic world. Not so long ago, aquarium tanks were relatively small affairs, peered at through window-like openings in the wall. Today's aquariums, however, have impossibly huge tanks where awesome volumes of water press at us with awesome force through layers of acrylic tens of centimetres thick.

To see through walls like this represents a major paradigm shift, as different as architectural elevations and cross-sections. When looking through a window, the view beyond is inviolate, self-contained. Not so with a transparent wall; an environment that ought to permeate everywhere suddenly cuts off at an invisible boundary, leaving its sheared face fully exposed. A visit to the aquarium in days gone by was like going to the circus; now one is fully immersed in the experience.

Thanks to these new aquariums, we now have a clearer image of aquatic life: how the underwater plants and animals move in ways unimaginable above ground, particularly in deeper, previously inaccessible waters, where the increased water pressure makes the deep-sea swimmers lethargic, the swaying fronds heavy. Like the subdued dramatics of Noh theatre, all is continuous movement caught in a slow-motion time warp, each cell and body part suspended at half-speed. Moreover, the reduced transparency of water shows everything as if through a silk curtain. A gauze-like diffusion that sets the reality of things off at a fixed distance. One loses the vital physicality; we see glazed fruits floating in a gelatine universe.

In one project currently under construction, my initial image was of an aquatic scene. Sited in the very heart of the city, facing onto an avenue lined with large beautiful cedars, a transparent cubic volume rises seven storeys from a 50m by 50m square ground plan. Seven thin floor-layers are supported by thirteen tube-like structures, each irregular non-geometric tube resembling a tree root, thicker towards the top as it nears the soil surface, splaying and bending slightly. These hollow tubes are sheathed in a basketry of plaited steel piping, mostly covered in frosted glass. The effect is like hollow translucent candles.

In the margin beside my first sketches for these tubes I wrote: "Columns like seaweed." I had imagined soft tubes slowly swaying underwater, hose-like volumes filled with fluid. Without resorting to the typical wall with windows – no glass façade dividing the building from the street, no clear acrylic plate out of a massive fish tank – I wanted to express the cut face to another world.

But why the aquatic image for a building on solid ground? For one thing, water is the primal shape-giver, the source of all life forms. Trees, for example, as they branch out recursively from trunk to twig to leaf tip resemble nothing so much as rivers that gather tributary streams and empty into the sea. The thick opacity of the trunk dividing into ever-finer branches, gradually forming an intricate membrane, and finally attaining the near-transparency of the leaves – the very image of fluidity.

If this is true of a tree growing above ground, how much more fluid then are those plants and animals that exist under water? Their very forms embody such movement. As with fish fins, those parts that suggest movement become more transparent towards the tip. Motion and form meet in fluidity; and fluidity is always translucent-to-transparent.

EROTIC TRANSPARENCY

Translucent objects always seem to be in transition from opaque to transparent. I am reminded of the metamorphosis of insects: the transparent larvae just out of their hard pupae are covered with a milky liquid; then, in an instant, contact with air turns them into adult insects with hard, clear wings. A half-formed translucent gel state stirs transformative imaginings; the moment it turns transparent and solid and fixed, that ambiguous fascination is lost.

Certain architecture, such as the early works of Mies van der Rohe, almost attain such gelatinous, near-liquid transparency. Known as the creator of transparent glass-and-steel twentieth-century architecture, Mies at the beginning of his career built with opaque materials – brick and stone. Then suddenly in the 1920s, his architecture undergoes a metamorphosis. In sketches for "Glass Skyscrapers" and the interior of the Barcelona Pavilion, fluid translucent spaces truly come to life.

The Barcelona Pavilion, the German pavilion at the 1921 Barcelona World's Fair, was steel in structure, but stone and glass gave it its flamboyant dynamism. The stone mosaic covering the abstract planar formation of the walls describes a boldly fluid wave pattern. Poised between these stone-faced walls, greenish frosted glass screens give the impression of tanks of water. The various planes play across at right angles, but never actually intersect. Rather, they overlap with the shallow outdoor pool surfaces to create a fluid space: the very image of solid form slowly melting into a liquid state. A most erotic space.

Similarly, the Japanese designer Shiro Kuramata was keenly attuned to such transparency in contemporary society, and actually pursued it in his creative work – very intuitively, at times playing the "villain" of bad taste. From the start of his career in the 1960s, he frequently used clear acrylic in his furniture designs. In one of his acrylic chairs, the furniture-object virtually disappears, leaving only the "primitive" act of sitting. His clean wardrobes and bureau-dressers were even more powerful in this respect in that storage, the act of putting things away, is essentially one of hiding objects in opaque, unseen places. But here, far from hiding them, the clothes on hangers and folded garments are displayed in floating space. The material box forms vanish and only the act of storage remains – in an erotically charged space, we might add. The effect of his transparent touch was not unlike trespassing in some forbidden room, catching a glimpse of what one is not supposed to see.

Three years before his death, one particular Kuramata design made a direct gesture to the eroticism of the transparent. The clear acrylic chair "Miss Blanche" (1988) achieved heightened transparency through artificial roses scattered in its "empty" interior. The red petals float this way and that as if drifting in a stream; floral patterns released from the heavy upholstery fabrics of old and turned into real flowers suspended in clear, liquid space.

Whereas making things transparent ought to be the most abstract of acts, a divesting of form into pure space, suddenly there appears an all-too-real, seductive presence. This polarity, these startling reversals, this real-unreal ambiguity are distinctly transparent tastes.

OPAQUE TRANSPARENCY

Transparency, however, is not always so light and clear. We Japanese have willingly sur-rendered any opacity of self so as to blend into today's society. We live see-through lives, undistinguished from anyone else in an extremely streamlined regulatory system. Urban Japan has become a convenience store peopled by instant snack foods wrapped in plastic and lined up on a shelf. We are mere signs, wholly transparent, devoid of any scale of value. What's more this mediocre transparent existence is entirely comfortable. And yet, as the individual in contemporary society turns ever more transparent, architecture and the city are becoming conversely more opaque.

One major characteristic of the contemporary city is that each space is utterly cut off from the next. Interiors partitioned room from room, walls everywhere. Such perhaps is the destiny of social control: a vast homogenised cityscape is fragmented into places with almost no spatial interrelationships. This is especially true in commercial spaces, where divorcing the interior from the external environment facilitates dramatically "staging" the premises. Spaces thick with shining product are clearly set up, when seen from a slight remove, on the basis of their uniformity and particularity; spaces seemingly so idiosyncratic are merely the accumulations of introspectively inflated fragments of homogeneity – this is today's city.

Walking through Shinjuku or Shibuya Station, two of the most complex spatial configurations in central Tokyo, is a very strange experience. All the criss-crossed levels of communication, intersecting train and subway lines, the three-dimensional knots of interlinking pedestrian passage ways between, commercial spaces surrounding and interpenetrating and surmounting this maze, everything is designed to make us lose our way inside a viewless world almost entirely cut off from the outside. All we have to go on are signs and verbalised cues. While we are in the midst of this complicated spatial experience, it is all we can do to create a correspondingly abstract and semiotic mental space.

A half-formed translucent gel state stirs transformative imaginings; the moment it turns solid and fixed, that ambiguous fascination is lost

What is demanded of today's architect is to discover "relationships" between such hermetic, fragmented spaces; to seek opaque-yet-transparent connections between multilayered spaces. In a project commissioned by one Japanese city, a Fire Department completed two years ago, I tried to realize an "opaque transparency." Almost all functional aspects of the building were raised on rows of columns to the upper storey. This so-called *pilotis* structure allowed the ground floor to maintain a continuity with the street in the form of a park-like space left open and accessible to all. The only provision is that a dozen or more fire trucks and ambulances and various pieces of training equip-ment be kept there as well. In the middle of a turfed area, two tower structures – large and small – are strung with climbing ropes and a long rope bridge between for the fire brigade's daily exercises. There is also a drowning-rescue practice pool and a small gym. The townspeople can drop by and watch the firefighters go through their paces; meanwhile the corridors connecting the individual rooms on the upper storey look down onto whatever is going on below. There are even lightwells through the upper storey floor to allow communication between levels. All this is designed to give the fire brigade a "face" in the daily life of the town, not just in the event of an emergency.

The building is not by any means glassed-in or transparent. However, openings here and there in the floor make for a certain dynamic between levels above and below – what I call "opaque transparency." Glass buildings are not the only way to achieve transparency; the task on hand today is how to forge relations between otherwise walled-off spaces.

In *The Mathematics of the Ideal Villa and Other Essays*,[1] Colin Rowe terms such relations "phenomenal transparency" as opposed to "literal transparency." In the title essay he cites by way of "phenomenal" examples the early works

> We are mere signs, wholly transparent, devoid of any scale of value

of Le Corbusier or the paintings of Fernand Léger; and as "literal" examples the Bauhaus architecture of Walter Gropius and the artworks of Laszlo Moholy-Nagy. In other words, while the latter is merely composed of transparent elements, the former layers non-transparent "blind" elements so as to create transparent interrelationships. Take, for instance, Le Corbusier's famous early work, the Villa

Stein at Garches (1927) and its abstract layering overlapping vertical and horizontal planes. The effect is such that despite the actual volume of the physical building, the composition becomes a Cubist painting with planes of no visual depth advancing and receding in non-Euclidian space.

Now more than ever, architecture must deliver such spatial relationships. For despite our apparent transparency, like all-too-colourless products lined up in a convenience store, we continue to build ever more solid barriers between us. Not that we should return to the world-without-walls collective existence of times past – even if we could. The key lies in introducing new openings through the walls we have already built.

Notes:
[1] MIT, Cambridge, 1976

Odate Jukai Dome, Akita, Japan. Photo: Mikio Kamaya ▶

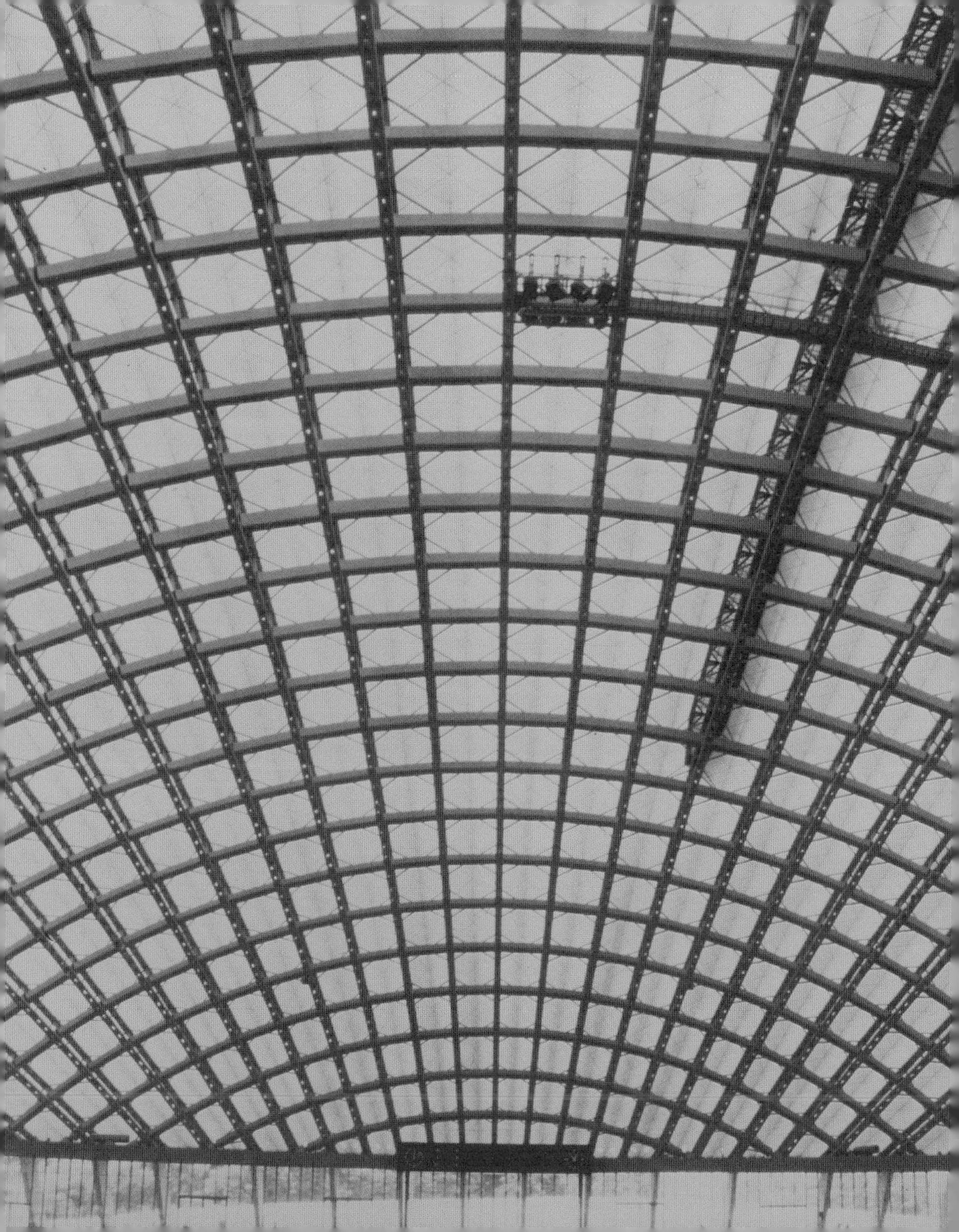

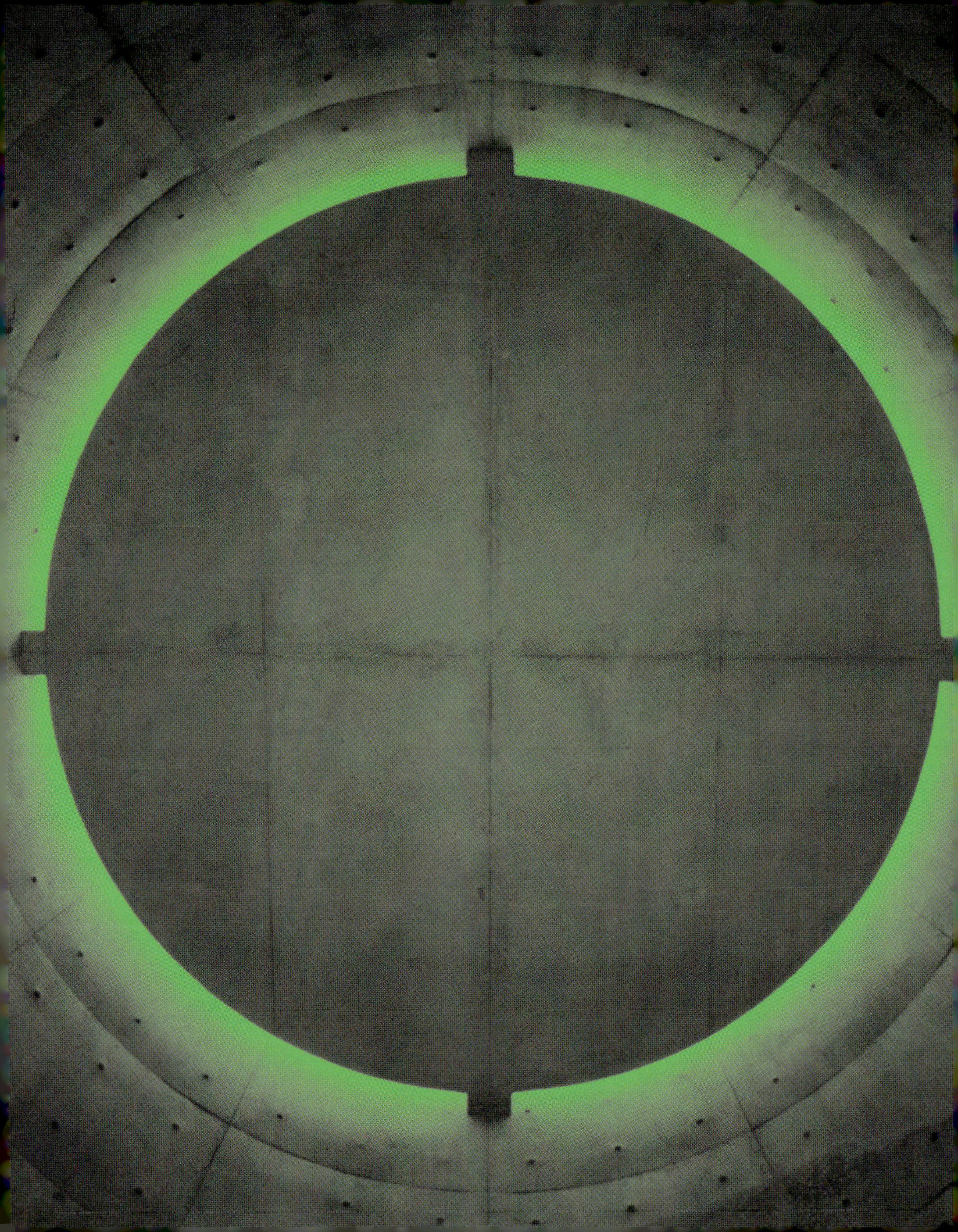

◄ Meditation Space, UNESCO, Paris

TADAO ANDO

Beyond Minimalism

The spirit is the core of the immeasurable; through a variety of processes thoughts are transformed into sketches, plans and drawings, and thus given expression

As we enter the twenty-first century, we are all too aware of the rapid change taking place throughout the world, not only in the natural and man-made environments but also, and most importantly, in our sense of values. Countries around the globe are obsessed by economics and, deluded by the idea that wealth creation embodies high values, have embraced a lifestyle run by computers and informed unquestioningly by mass media. We have lost sight of the truly important things in life.

If this trend continues, the differences between our cultures will be blended into homogeneous uniformity, which will destroy the characteristics of traditions that each nation or people has inherited. It will kill the sense of association to a specific region, the moral and spiritual character in its roots, and even the individual races themselves.

In the countries of the Asian region especially, the economy has been given major emphasis in political and social policy. Material aspects have been unduly glorified; the indigenous culture, the traditions and history of each region have been ignored and even scorned. It would, however, be difficult to stem the flow of this trend which is running with the tide of the times. Even in architecture the volume of unnecessary information, the speed of its dissemination and the trend towards homogeneity, reinforced by economic reasoning, are a powerful presence. Architects must be consciously aware of these pressures and reflect on where their real responsibilities lie.

> The most important aspect of architecture is its ability to move people with its poetic and creative power

I should like to reaffirm that the most important aspect of architecture is its ability to move people with its poetic and creative power, and also to raise again the question of whether architecture can be a true culture in and of itself.

I should like to think that the interaction of architecture with nature can awaken and revive people's sensitivities through their physical being and their senses and can arouse in people the perceptiveness that they intrinsically possess. If we assume that what makes architecture true "Architecture" is not just a specific plan or design, not its relationship to technique or cost, but its aesthetic expression of the architect's awareness of the issues involved, then the definition lies not only in architecture as a completed structure but within the process that is involved in its creation, in the manner in which it acquires life. The processes which take place before the architecture is born as form, while it is being converted into reality, and the change which occurs with time once it has been finished, are all part of this act of creation. It is during that process of transition from poetic inspiration to the creation of form that the full range of an architect's ideas and thinking is brought to action. It is through repeated deliberation and contemplation, by searching every which way, by trial and error that the creative process which leads to architectural expression can be intensified and become profound.

Thought is the realm where the soul and spirit are one. The spirit is the core of the immeasurable; through a variety of processes thoughts are transformed into sketches, plans and drawings, and thus given expression. If, when my ideas or concepts progress – and within each line drawn, each number, each mark and symbol, or even the space in between, is injected the history, tradition, spiritual character and the sense of regional association to which my body and my five senses are deeply connected – if it can then acquire an eminence of aesthetic poetics, then I think it would truly become "Architecture."

Twentieth-century architecture consists of techniques and materials – steel, concrete, glass, aluminium – that are common the world over. This tends to make buildings around the globe essentially the same and, like a dull and repetitious lifestyle, mundane and boring. It is incumbent on us to use the resources of our Earth in a more diverse manner; we should respect the unique lifestyles that are born from the differences in our cultures. I deliberately resist the idea of a "shrinking Earth." There is no reason, despite its use of common materials and techniques, for modern archi-tecture in Asian countries, the United Kingdom, Europe or the United States to be exactly the same and in an age of spreading digital information and globalization, architects must address their responsibilities in a number of areas, the most important of which is what value we are to place on culture. The basis of culture is the moral and spiritual characteristics, the sensibilities, that a people have inherited through the ages. This is in addition to language and to the sense of association to nation or region. I therefore believe it is important that we use architecture to carry into the twenty-first century the covenant of culture that has been passed down to us through so much adversity.

> It is important that we use architecture to carry into the twenty-first century the covenant of culture that has been passed down to us through so much adversity

In this period of accelerating globalization we must make a conscious effort to preserve the peculiar language, the aesthetic values and the sensibilities that constitute the root of a culture as well as the almost unconscious physical habits that we inherit and use in our daily lives and also the craftsmanship that is handed down to us, all of which may be considered to be the true strength and power of a people. Language is deeply connected to a people's moral and spiritual make-up; writing and speaking in that language determine their form of expression.

For a piece of architecture to possess a universality that is understood through a common consciousness in people of all races and beliefs, it must be understood through the process of thought and planning that takes place before its completion. The intrinsic culture, tradition, history, the moral and spiritual character of a people is intimately entwined in the process of deliberation and will determine whether or not the architect's understanding of these issues will reach the heights of architectural expression. Thus do I reaffirm my conviction that any consideration of architecture must be centred on the process of creation itself.

▲ Garden of Fine Arts, Kyoto – Layered facets of light and shadow

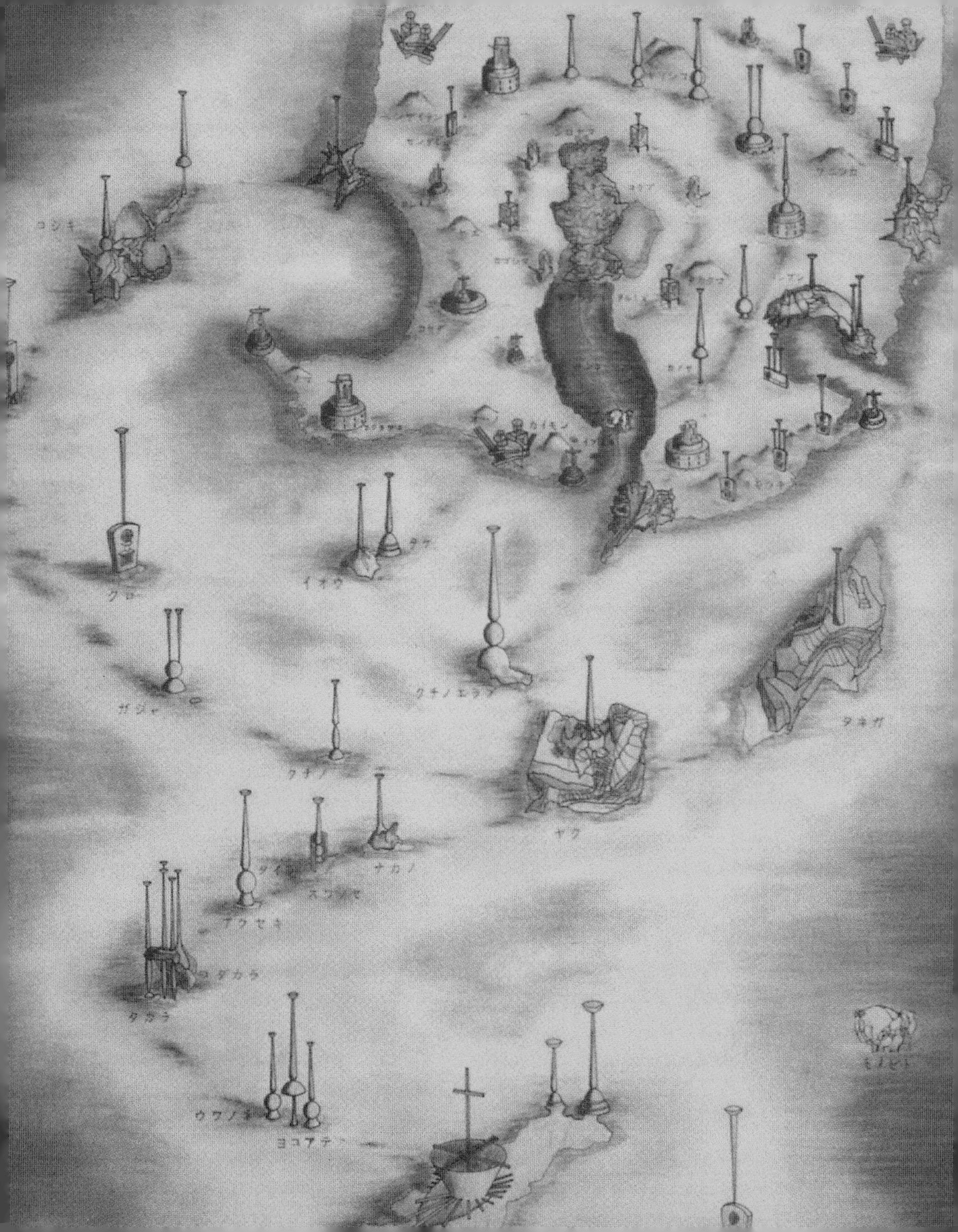
コシキ
クロ
イオウ
タケ
ガジャ
クチノエラブ
クチノ
ヤク
タネガ
ナカノ
スワノセ
アクセキ
コダカラ
タカラ
ヨコアテ

MASAHARU TAKASAKI

Kagoshima Cosmology

Today Kagoshima is no more than a sacred place. It is one of several places in the prefecture where the peculiar culture to which shamanism belongs is still alive today

In Kagoshima Prefecture, which lies at the most south-westerly tip of Japan, there is a volcanic mountain range which consists of Sakurajima, Kirishima and Kaimondake. Sakurajima, especially, which erupts even today, is a symbol of the dynamism of this land. In this particular environment there is also the East China Sea to the West, the Pacific Ocean to the south-east and south, and also many large and small islands that deserve attention. The imported cultures came with the flow of the Black Current – the southern character that has the power to stimulate even the hardened spirit of today's people. The Ocean, as calm as a mirror of still water, keeps the awesome energy of the volcano deep underground. The peculiar land form relates with the energy of fire, soil and water, existing with pride and exuding an impression of indescribable spirituality.

Today Kagoshima is no more than a sacred place. One can imagine from such topographical characteristics that it is the absolute place with an abundance of affection for ancient times, without respect for its history, where the myths of Deity come down. It is one of several places in the prefecture where the peculiar culture to which shamanism belongs is still alive today.

Some may have the same feelings about the place through strange imaginings. In my case, I feel a great burst of energy when I sense the power of the land where the energy of fire, soil and water, is rife. This feeling is like communicating with an inner world beyond visible communication, this sensitive communication of a consciousness of primeval human nature. It is a similar feeling to the moment when our consciousness is overcome or our soul stunned by the appearance of a sacred phantom. That momentary floating feeling is similar to the separation of the body from the soul. The land, longing for ancient times, like a topographic Mandala, intuitively penetrates the hard shell of modern civilization.

Why has such a configuration appeared here? There are many such places in Kagoshima that show their strong will to be there. I do not know any other place like this land, which strengthens so much my yearning for its original topography. In Kagoshima, the ancient and the present coexist and there is a mystery in which the imagination comes unconsciously. It is the sacred illusion, drawn from reaction to the imagination, that goes beyond theory and technique. It is a provocation against super-modernism. The ancient energy, which flows through and all over the topographic Mandala always connects with a future one thousand years later. The history of Kagoshima from primeval times is not yet complete; the energy in the volcano range has an inner rhythm of returning to the past and moving towards the future concurrently. It might have to react to the sacred rhythm of energy to create the utopia of Kagoshima Cosmology today. Kagoshima Cosmology, which emerges from consideration of a phantom, could coordinate the opposite vectors of the past and the future and would only become a present day Utopia in a place where its essence is found through the ages, both ancient and future.

I am searching for a kind of architecture that would be suitable for such a sacred place. In my first project in Kagoshima – Zero Cosmology – the zero form emanates from the phantom where ancient feeling and the future coexist, and the symbolic small cosmos of Kagoshima Cosmology is an actual Utopia as if by revelation. In that universal egg, the zero as eternal life, deathless time runs along. All things come around with

> I feel a great burst of energy when I sense the power of the land where the energy of fire, soil and water, is rife

timeless essence and subconscious matters are accepted. I shall continue to cling to the floating feeling of architecture here in Kagoshima as if the architecture has come to flee the future. A style giving an impression of floating is my idea for architecture in Kagoshima. The absolute land, which is calling out to ancient times, is wounded by our current blunt civilization and looks to the future while it considers ancient times. My architecture will continue to reject landing here, in the present. The architecture exists in the present but it is absent from this era and goes to other places or times. The presence of architecture stimulates the human sub-conscious. A mysterious world is created in the Utopia in the subconscious. It is towards this fantasy that architecture should aim spiritually.

Sacred places invite holy architecture. To respond to the invitation of the Deity, it is necessary to foretell the situation one thousand years in the future. Architecture should land on earth as if it came from a distant universe. The appearance of architecture means not only architecture anchored in the present but also architecture anchored in history. The paradise of Kagoshima Cosmology has appeared vividly in the consciousness of space.

In the topographical Mandala of Kagoshima, there is much in nature that looks as if it was designed by God. For instance, *The Standing God in the Office* of Amami Osima is a large rock standing in the sea and it is the "place of God," drawn in the Mandala. In addition, it is the place where the shaman might say, "Oh God please be seated here." It would be the fantasy of architecture, the coincidence of existence and absence deeply connected with human consciousness. "Oh God, please be seated here," the shaman's voice echoes in my timeless illusion. Kagoshima Cosmology is the true home of architecture.

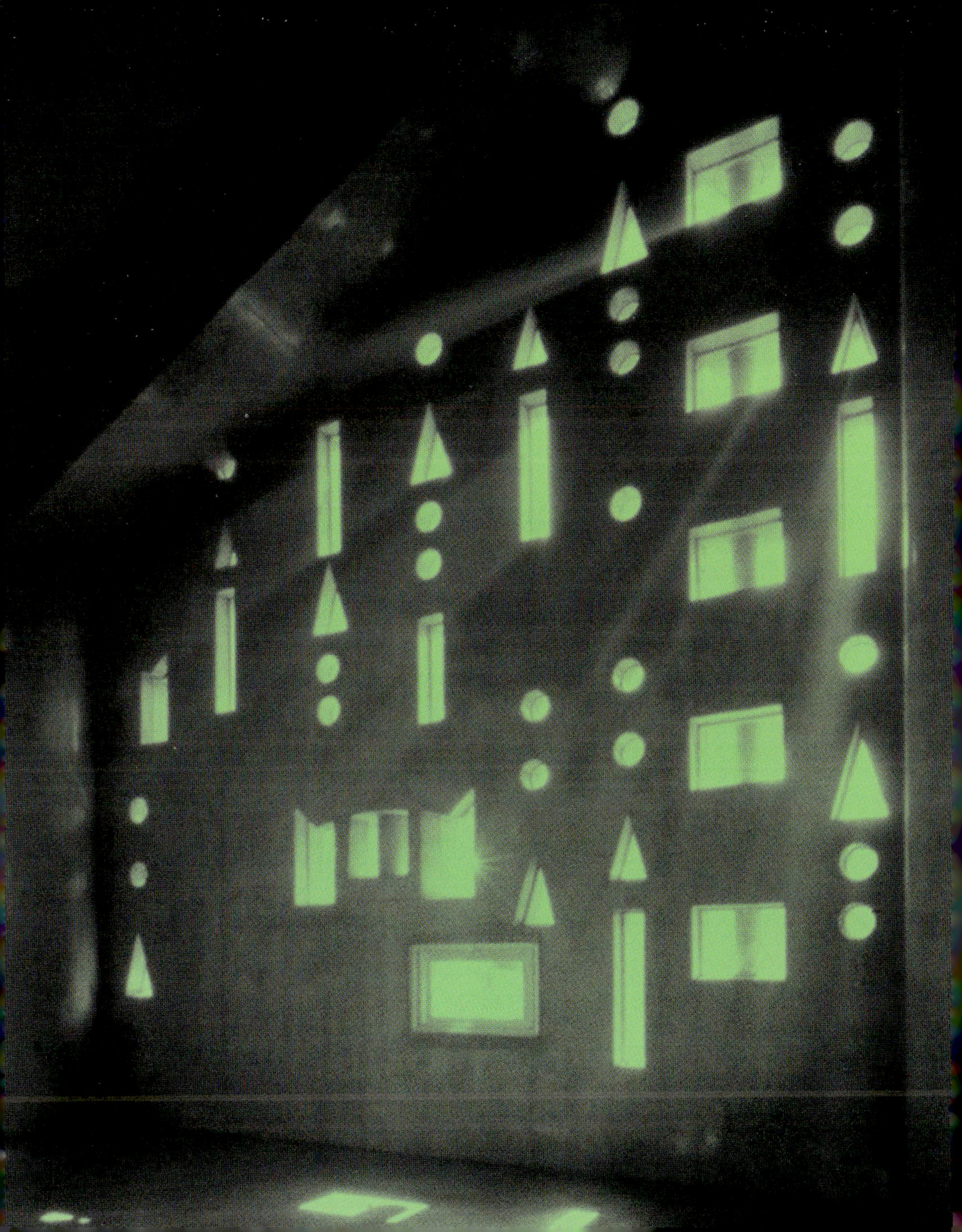

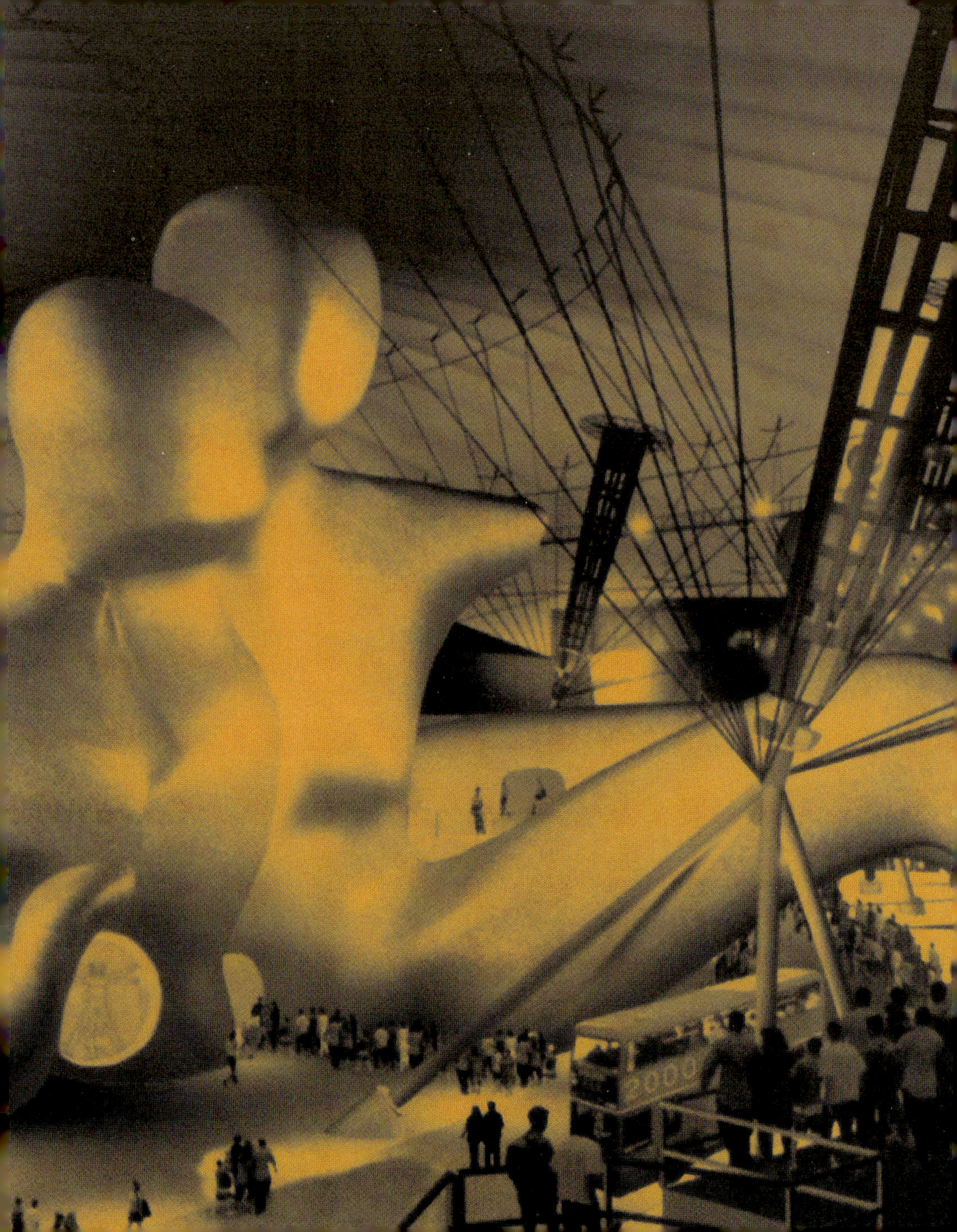
2000

◄ The Body Zone, the Millennium Dome by Nigel Coates
Photo: Peter Goodeve

BERNARD TSCHUMI
ON NIGEL COATES

Bodies From Outer Space

*What better story to express at this scale than the body?
Although it is huge, I hope that everyone who sees it somehow sees
themselves in it; when they have been through it, that they feel
charged up to do more with their own bodies*

Nigel Coates

1. It is amusing to notice how much the human body seems to perplex architects and architectural historians. First seen as part of a static system of proportional relations (Leonardo's diagram), later the body was viewed occasionally as a dynamic set of forces in transit through architectural space (choreographies of bodies in space). Rarely was the morphology of the body addressed literally by architects as a starting point for their work.

○

2. More recently, it became no less amusing to notice how biological analogies and biomorphic images informed recent computer generated architecture. But the veins, arteries, and lungs that populate the current vocabulary of architectural forms seem to carefully avoid the human body itself. Maybe the body, by being too "human" is therefore not architectural.

○

3. "The Body" conceived by Nigel Coates and his friends for the Millennium Dome interests me insofar as it seems to succeed in collapsing the Renaissance's proportional relations, bodies in motion and biomorphic impulses all into one. If blobs are said to come from outer space, this blob comes from our space – the Earth – and therefore assumes a human form. Or does it? We witness the morphing of two figures into one, the streamlining of all irrelevant and cumbersome detailing: after all, an ear and all its folds are no doubt too earthly to be compatible with the future dynamics of mutants.

4. I would be tempted to consider that this highly polished human figure is not from the Earth, but is an alien figure from outer space that has assumed bodily characteristics to fool us, to make us believe that it is a familiar sight we should not be afraid of. Think: the skin is made of a strange material that changes colour as you approach it; each curve is mapped carefully according to sophisticated computer geometries. The earthly visitors undergo a fantastic voyage as they penetrate through some unspecified (again derived from outer space) orifice, only to be expelled smoothly a few minutes later from another hole, back onto the earth.

5. It could be the first built blob building of architecture.

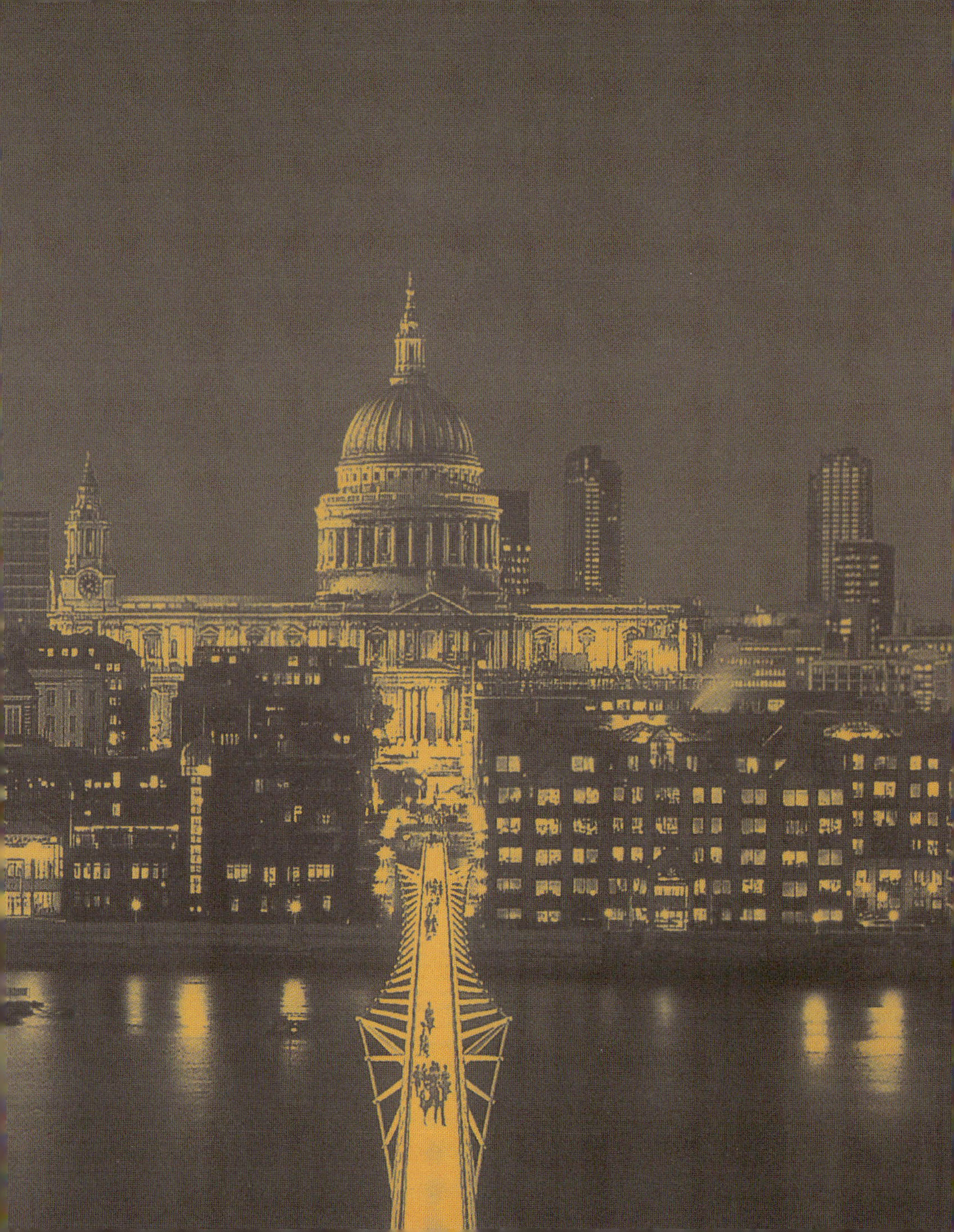

◀ Night view of the Millennium Bridge with St. Paul's Cathedral in the background
Photomontage. Photograph Hayes Davidson / Jeremy Young

KEN POWELL

Norman Foster's Triumph

Foster is arguably the architect of the millennium, rivaling James Stirling as the most influential British architect of the twentieth century and combining commercial success with artistic acclaim

For Norman Foster, the twentieth century ended with a flourish. At the millennium, his practice is not only the most prestigious in Britain – it is also one of the largest and most profitable. On the world scene, Foster is critically ranked alongside Piano and Gehry, Meier and Ando, Siza and Moneo – as the recent their practice, however, none of these figures can quite equal Foster. He is arguably the architect of the millennium, rivaling James Stirling, his sometime teacher and mentor, as the most influential British architect of the twentieth century and combining commercial success with artistic acclaim to a degree which Lutyens would have thought inconceivable.

The phenomenal success of Foster and Partners is guaranteed to engender envy and sheer malice, particularly in Britain – where quantity and quality are seen as irreconcilables. Hence the gleeful jibes about French stone (at the time of a "beef war") used at the British Museum, of all places, the media campaign to find fault with the Berlin Reichstag (perhaps the most difficult project Foster has ever tackled) and the prominence given to the Foster projects which allegedly reflect a slipping of standards and are the work of a "B" team at his office. Such is the potency of the Foster legend, however, that the deficiencies of such schemes are often blamed on an inadequate input from the great man himself. Foster's personal charisma and sheer energy remain central to the office's success, something which even SOM in its greatest years, in the 1950s and 1960s, never possessed.

Foster's reputation was first forged back in the 1960s, when he was a partner with Richard Rogers in Team 4. The two men remain good friends, but their partnership was an unlikely one. Neither is content to share the starring role. For nearly twenty years, since the time of the Hong Kong & Shanghai Bank project, in fact, Norman Foster has depended on a small group of fellow directors to make his potentially unwieldy operation work. Most prominent amongst them is Spencer de Grey, whom Foster took back to London as his lieutenant when the other directors were all committed to a long stint in Hong Kong. De Grey, the son of a former President of the Royal Academy, is an adept negotiator, a flawless presenter of projects and a forceful team manager – Foster still depends greatly on his expertise and judgement. Equally vital to the practice, in their different ways, are the other members of the core group – David Nelson, Graham Phillips and Ken Shuttleworth. "Key individuals will still play a decisive role in the field of design," Foster predicted some thirty years ago while extolling the merits of teamwork. De Grey, Nelson, Phillips, and Shuttleworth are all "key individuals," a role which a number of younger directors of Foster and Partners are also increasingly assuming. The Foster magic is, to no small degree, about good management and a wise use of resources.

It is also, as much as ever, about Norman Foster's personal and passionate sense of conviction and even of mission. He could never be a titular president or figurehead. He needs to be involved in the process of design. Given the scale of the practice today, however, his role in a project is often confined to that of initiator of ideas and critical reviewer. He is the individual who sees, on occasions, that a scheme is going wrong, has lost direction, who works late into the night with the team to get it right. Foster is determined still that everything that leaves the office bears a distinctive mark of quality and innovation – he sees open-mindedness and the refusal to produce stock solutions as Foster and Partners' greatest strength. He is genuinely wounded by charges that the office produces "ordinary" work. Everything it does, he believes, should be extraordinary. In other words, he sets himself a colossal task. Now in his mid sixties, he shows no signs of retreating from practice: the support he gets from an unusually happy marriage underpins his professional life. Unlike his old friend (and fellow life peer) Richard Rogers, who has been drawn into New Labour politics and environmental campaigning, Foster has no wish to enter public life beyond the world of architecture and urbanism. His outlook is pragmatic, conservative even. The United States which so impressed him as a young man, a confident, capitalist country, with "can do" as its prime motto, is still part of his philosophy of life. If Foster keeps his younger colleagues working late into the night, developing a project, he can remind them of when he was their age and the legendary Paul Rudolph – still very much a Foster hero – scheduled design sessions at Yale for 3 am! Born into a poor family in Manchester, Foster is unapologetic about enjoying the material fruits of success, though his executive jet, he insists, is a resource for the office and vital to his personal schedule. Much of Foster's own work on projects is done these days at his house in the south of France, with other team members periodically flown out to work with him. The Reichstag was one project to which Foster's personal input at all levels, from the political and strategic down to detailed design issues, was absolutely critical.

The Reichstag is one of the most striking expressions of Foster's internationalism. Even more than Richard Rogers' earlier success in the Pompidou Centre competition – achieved in partnership with an Italian – Foster's victory in that for the Hong Kong & Shanghai Bank in 1979 marked the break with the old imperial concerns of British architecture and the advent of a new globalism. Foster Associates (as the practice was then titled) was transformed over the next decade from a leading-edge London atelier into a world business.

Even as the Hong Kong Bank was rising, Foster Associates was working on competitions in Italy, France, Germany, the USA, Japan and Mexico – where the Televisa HQ project was to become an important source for many later projects. Televisa remained unbuilt, but many projects were brought to fruition – the Carré d'Art in Nimes (1984-93, for example, an expression of Foster's growing interest in urban design), the Barcelona Tower (1988-92), the stations for the Bilbao Metro (1988-95 and continuing), a group of buildings in Duisburg (1988-97), and the Commerzbank in Frankfurt (1991-97), a job which was significant when it came to the contest for the Reichstag.

The year 1991 was an *annus mirabilis* for Foster. Knighted the previous year, he saw six important projects completed, including the widely applauded terminal at Stansted (begun on site in 1987), the Sackler Galleries at the Royal Academy, and the Crescent Wing at the Sainsbury Centre, Norwich. By 1991, however, the British economy was deep in recession and foreign shores beckoned more invitingly than ever. During the following year, Foster secured two commissions which were to dominate the office for some years, the Reichstag and the new Chek Lap Kok airport in Hong Kong.

> Foster is genuinely wounded by charges that the office produces "ordinary" work. Everything it does, he believes, should be extraordinary

In theory, the Chek Lap Kok scheme, developed by a consortium of which Foster and Partners was one element, was a design and build scheme, yet it bears the typical Foster imprint of quality and consistency. Reportedly one of the few man-made structures which can be seen from the Moon, the new airport terminal building (which opened in 1998) occupies a specially constructed island, six kilometres long, and is expected to handle up to ninety million passengers annually when the projected second phase is completed. The scheme builds on the lessons of the far smaller Stansted terminal, notably in creating a huge and immediately impressive public space through which all passengers, departing or arriving, must pass. Modern travel is characterised by routine, the absence of any sense of adventure or drama – indeed, by a sense that the traveller is merely a commodity being processed. Foster has always fought to instil a new drama into travel, so that the Hong Kong terminal has a powerful sense of direction and movement as passengers are drawn through lofty, barrel-vaulted spaces from the great atrium into the wings of the building. Using a combination of concrete and steel, Foster gives the interiors a dynamic lightness which is both symbolic and highly practical.

Foster's "continuing process of discovery, inspiration, invention and innovation," cited by the jury of the 1999 Pritzker Prize, is genuine and is applied to a staggering range of projects, great and small. The Berlin Reichstag (1992-99) drew on all of Foster's strengths. The choice of the old Reichstag building (badly damaged by the 1933 fire and by wartime shelling and rather perfunctorily rebuilt in the 1960s) as the new home of the German Federal Parliament posed immediate issues of how far such a monument of the "old" Germany should or could be restored. It was Santiago Calatrava who first came up with the idea of a reinstated dome (though not a copy of the lost dome). The lack of such a feature appeared to be the only deficiency in Foster's competition scheme, which was otherwise the strongest contender.

Foster's incorporation of a dome into the scheme appears, in retrospect, effortless, yet it involved much thought and self-questioning. Determined not to build a meaningless token of homage to the past, Foster developed the dome, in the spirit of his supreme mentor, Buckminster Fuller, as a source of natural light and ventilation. It also became a symbol not of hierarchy and enclosure (like that of the Kaiserist Reichstag) but of democracy and openness, a tourist attraction, a place where you could go merely to enjoy the view, a people's place. It was a daring move and there were many critics, not only on the right – the retention of the graffiti left by victorious Russian soldiers in 1945 infuriated some conservatives. It is too early to assess the success of the building in use, yet Foster's dome has become a familiar and popular feature of the Berlin skyline, an

> Foster's "continuing process of discovery, inspiration, invention and innovation", is genuine and is applied to a staggering range of projects, great and smal.
> *Cited by the jury of the 1999 Pritzker Prize*

important public monument in a city where new office towers dominate.

Back in Britain, Foster spent the second half of the 1990s balancing commercial work against major public commissions including the Millennium Bridge (designed with sculptor Sir Anthony Caro and engineer Chris Wise of Ove Arup), the Greater London Authority building, the British Museum Great Court, and the World Squares initiative. He also turned his attention increasingly to provincial Britain, with projects as far-flung as Scotland, Gateshead and west Wales. Not that international jobs fell off. The recent commission from the Museum of Fine Arts in Boston – particularly welcome in view of Norman Foster's continuing love affair with America, where he has only one completed work (and that in Nebraska) – confirms Foster's standing in the field of arts and education, while the practice is a big player in the global commercial field, as its haul of current projects in Korea, China, Australia and in major European cities confirms. Ten years ago, Foster's office had a turnover of £8 million. A decade later, this had quadrupled and in 1998 it had a payroll of 500 – a total which has since fallen somewhat.

One of Foster's perennial dilemmas is continuing to infuse innovation and experiment into the practice's work. It is Foster, for example, who, inspired by the example of Buckminster Fuller, has personally pushed the "green" environmental agenda – "it is not about fashion but about survival," he insists. The low energy Frejus school (1991) was an important landmark in this aspect of the office's work, with the use of a double cavity roof to create a solar chimney effect and generous sunshading used to architectural effect. It was Foster who committed a team to the development of a solar-powered vehicle and has been an active supporter of the international solar power programme which reflects his belief in the benign potential of technology, responsibly used. Foster has said of Buckminster Fuller (with whom he worked on various unbuilt projects between 1968 and 1983) that "he made you believe that anything is possible." The element of aspiration – a visionary element, even – has never been far removed from Foster's own work.

It is hard to imagine how Fuller would have reacted to a project like the Reichstag. Since Foster completed the Willis Faber headquarters in Ipswich a quarter of a century ago – a highly original response to a historic urban quarter – architects have been increasingly drawn into the masterplanning of towns and cities and increasingly obliged to respond, positively and sympathetically, to history. For Foster, the Carré d'Art was undoubtedly a turning point in terms of working with the past – he was the only one of a group of eminent contenders for the commission who really embraced the exquisite Maison Carrée and sought to give it a meaningful new setting. The Royal Academy Sackler Galleries scheme was another landmark, showing how restoration and radical new design could co-exist and certainly offering a vignette, in due course, of the potential of the Reichstag. Another massive project which traces its ancestry back to the Sackler Galleries is the British Museum Great Court, set to create the largest covered public space in Europe under an ethereal lightweight steel and glass roof (and one of a group of plum Lottery projects won by Foster and Partners). Foster envisages this space as open to all, late into the evening, part of the public domain – like the World Squares project which he skilfully captured from Richard Rogers (whose campaigning, ironically, had fuelled the idea of taming traffic and creating pedestrian-friendly spaces at the heart of London). Two of the best of Foster's unbuilt projects, the Hammersmith transport interchange (1977) and BBC Radio Headquarters (1985) can be seen as pioneering attempts, before their time, to extend and civilize the public domain. Foster's many years of work on the site around King's Cross and St Pancras stations in London – where he first tackled major urban planning issues – also ended inconclusively.

Foster is as likely to single out a door handle as an example of his approach to design as he is an airport or office tower. He delights in small projects – domestic interiors, for example, or the fitout of an exhibition on Modern Britain at London's Design Museum in which he personally (and unexpectedly) took a leading role. Some would claim that this sort of job is merely an escape from the routine of a large office. Foster and Partners is currently working on at least six sites in the City of London. It is building a tower at London's Canary Wharf to equal the existing tower by Cesar Pelli. It would be unrealistic to claim that all these projects embody the degree of innovation seen, for instance, at Willis Faber. Foster's partner, Spencer de Grey, responds to charges that the office is doing too much and pursuing quantity over quality – "our defence must be, if we need one, that we can do these jobs better than other architects – we never compromise on quality."

Few of these schemes, in fact, fit easily into the traditional image of "HighTech" design. (The term is one which Foster has always disliked and rejected.) The Hong Kong Bank brought Foster close in spirit to the contemporary work of Richard Rogers – the project overlapped with Lloyd's of London – but its language of exposed structure and services did not persist in Foster's later work. "Calm" is a word which Foster tends to use, always positively, of his work. A feeling of calm and order fills the new Jubilee Line Extension station at Canary Wharf, opened late in 1999, as large as an airport terminal and intended to handle 25,000 passengers per hour. The station has real majesty and its sense of serenity is enhanced by the skilful use of daylight and, after dark, by the quietly dramatic lighting strategy devised by Foster's regular collaborator, Claude Engle. Not for Foster the more baroque sense of colour and form seen in Alsop's station across the river at North Greenwich. When Foster was pitted against Alsop in the competition for the new home of the Greater London Authority, it was not only the financial equations which impressed. (Foster's building was to form part of a massive office quarter which he was also masterplanning.) Alsop would have radically adapted an old building. Foster offered London a recognizable symbol of restored local government. The scheme went through various permutations, was compared, variously, to a glass testicle and a fencing mask, but is likely to become an instant landmark, as much a product of the Blairite era as the Dome.

In Bilbao to inspect his completed metro stations, Foster went to see the new Guggenheim Museum by Frank Gehry. He was immediately impressed and felt that the building was a masterpiece. Back in Britain, he has joined the lobby in favour of Daniel Libeskind's V&A "Spiral" building. Although stemming from a tradition which is not his, these projects are much to Foster's taste. In his own work, he is striving increasingly for strong and memorable form – witness the Duxford Air Museum, the Daewoo Tower in Seoul and the designs for the Swiss Re tower on the Baltic Exchange site in the City of London. The latter, Foster feels, could be as significant for the 2000s as was Willis Faber for the 1970s, incorporating as it does the low energy advances of the late twentieth century and a progressive approach to workplace design. The radicalism of the Swiss Re scheme – which looks increasingly likely to be built – compensates for the loss of the earlier Millennium Tower scheme projected for this key site.

Swiss Re could be seen as Norman Foster's attempt to rekindle the excitement of Willis Faber, to capitalize too on a public mood which has been radicalized by Gehry, Libeskind, and the visions of Future Systems. Sixty-five this year, with the Royal Gold Medal (which he won as early as 1983), the AIA Gold Medal and the Order of Merit – an extraordinary honour, granted to few architects – under his belt, Lord Foster is entitled to air his visions. In recent years, he has spoken eloquently of his sources of inspiration – Fuller, of course, Louis Kahn, Paul Rudolph, Serge Chermayeff, Ray and Charles Eames, and Frank Lloyd Wright, whose works he trekked across the United States in all weathers to see, more than thirty years ago, in company with Richard Rogers. And even before he went to America and found his way of designing, there was the Town Hall in Manchester, superficially an ornate work of the Gothic Revival but also a masterpiece of rational planning and integrated servicing. Foster has no qualms about revisiting his sources and, indeed, his own earlier works, stressing the connections between even the earliest works – the little glazed "cockpit" at Creek Vean, for example, or the Reliance Controls factory – and those currently at design stage.

Foster is, at heart, a rationalist in the same way that Richard Rogers is a romantic. It was Foster who came to admire the work of Mies van der Rohe. Rogers perceived its formal qualities, but not, in the end, its point. Mies impressed by his consistency. Superficially, at least, Foster has not been overly concerned with consistency. His work has been through a number of transformations and shows no signs of standing still as it responds to the context of place, culture and time. What consistency could there be between – and these are all Foster projects currently under construction – the National Botanic Garden of Wales, a prehistory museum in the Massif Central, a culture complex in Riyadh and a faculty block in Oxford? Foster's rationalism, universalist, maybe, at heart, has faced up to the diversity of the world at the millennium. How can the new Wembley Stadium be a purely rational, functional structure? It must express the often irrational excitement of mass spectator sport just as Stansted expresses the excitement of flying. Foster's work is in itself a microcosm of the world of architecture today. At its very core is a belief that the natural world, and the accumulated culture of the ages of which architecture forms a part, demands a great deal of the architecture of the future. Bolstered by the self-confidence that any great architect must have, an optimist through and through, but aware of the power of buildings to shape human life for better or worse, Foster is uniquely well equipped to play a central role in defining a continuing role for architects in the twenty-first century.

> Foster is, at heart, a rationalist in the same way that Richard Rogers is a romantic

Republished in "On Foster...Foster On" (Prestel)

KEN POWELL

◀ St Clement, 1998, from "The Ecstasy of Photography", a series of exhibitions of Baudrillard's photographs, featured in *Art and Artefact*, edited by Nicholas Zurbrugg (Sage Publications)

JEAN BAUDRILLARD

Truth and Radicality in Architecture

For me Photography has nothing to do with finding a particular vision or a subjective style in order to interpret the world. Rather, it is a process of capturing things, because objects are themselves captivating

Jean Baudrillard, from an interview with Nicholas Zurbrugg

Let us begin with space, which is after all the primal arena of architecture, and with the radicality of space, which is the void. Is it necessary, is it possible to structure, to organize this space other than by extending it indefinitely horizontally or vertically? In other words, when confronted with the radicality of space, can we invent truth in architecture?

Does architecture peter out in its reality, in its references, in its procedures, in its functions, in its techniques? Or does it go beyond all that and lose itself in something else, which is perhaps its own end, or something that might permit it to go beyond its own end? Does architecture exist beyond truth, beyond its own truth, in a sort of radicality that challenges space – rather than controls it – that challenges society in its obedience to its conventions and institutions, that challenges the very creation of architecture and the creative architect with his illusion of control.

I wanted to define architectural illusion in its two contradictory meanings: when it creates an illusion and is indeed itself an illusion; and when it invents a fresh illusion, a new illusion of the city and space, another arena where it exceeds its brief.

Personally, I am above all interested in space and in everything that in so-called built objects gives me a vertiginous sense of space. And so it is buildings such as the Pompidou Centre, the World Trade Center and Biosphere II that interest me, not because they are architectural masterpieces – it wasn't their architectural significance that captivated me – but the fact that, like the majority of our great contemporary architectural objects, they seem to have been parachuted from another world. What truth do they have? If, for example, I take the truth of a building like the two towers of the World Trade Center, I see that the architecture of that time, the 1960s, draws the profile of a hyperreal but not yet computerized society and period. The two towers already resemble two perforated cards in their twinness. Today we could say that they were already the sign, the clone of each other. Are they a precursor of our age? And in that case is the architect working not with reality but with fiction, in an anticipatory illusion of our society? Or is he simply translating what is already there? It is in this sense that I asked the question: is there truth in architecture in the sense of a suprasensible, intended purpose of architecture and space?

Let us try and see what there is in this creative illusion, in what is beyond reality in architecture. The architect's adventure takes place in a real world. He is in a particular situation that is not that of the traditional artist. He is not someone who pores over blank pages or a blank canvas. He has to create in a limited time, to a fixed budget, for specific people an object that is not always defined in advance. He works with a team in a situation where he has direct or indirect safety, financial and professional constraints.

Under these circumstances, what scope is there for freedom, for circumventing the constraints? The problem is to articulate each project according to a prior concept or idea using a very specific strategy to define a place that one does not know. We are in the field of invention, of non-knowledge, of risk and, in the end, this place can become a place of secrecy, of things not under control, which belong in the realm of fate or the voluntary surrender of control. This is where overt illusion comes into play: the illusion of a space which is not only visible but which may be the mental prolongation of what

> The architect's adventure takes place in a real world. He is not someone who pores over blank pages or a blank canvas

we see. The basic hypothesis here is that architecture is not what fills a space but what generates space, whether by misappropriation, by isolation, or by an almost unconscious conjuring trick. But from then on the mind plays its part. Take a Japanese garden, where there is always a vanishing point, a place where one does not know if the garden ends or continues. Or again, take Jean Nouvel's Tower without End for La Défense in Paris. It is an attempt to go beyond the logic of the Albertian perspective, in other words to organize all the elements in such a way that they can be read in a scale progression and make one conscious of space. The fact that the Tower disappears into the sky, goes beyond the boundary of the immaterial and is at the limits of the tangible and of perception is part of an architecture that is not virtual (although the Tower has remained virtual in that it has never been built). But it has created more than one can see. It is a seductive mental space for the eye and for the mind. In the Fondation Cartier, also by Jean Nouvel, the façade is larger than the building and I do not know if I am looking at the sky itself or at the sky through transparent glass. If I look at a tree through three layers of glass, I do not know whether I am looking at a tree through glass or at the reflection of a tree. And when two trees are lined up in relation to the glass, I do not know if there is a second tree and if it is a real tree.

This form of illusion is not gratuitous. Through the destabilisation of perception it permits the creation of a mental space, and the installation of a setting, a scenic space, without which, as we know, buildings would be merely constructions and the city itself an agglomeration of constructions. All our cities suffer from this loss of setting – and thus of the whole dramaturgy of illusion and seduction – because their space is filled with functional architecture, some useful some useless.

A presentation of the Issey Miyake collection at the Fondation Cartier provided a good illustration of the object in a stage setting, for the transparency of this architectural object gives it the role of an actor. Scene One – Issey Miyake's creations moving through the interior space. Then the gallery full of guests – the majority of them women in Issey Miyake – are also, without knowing it, part of the same scene. Then the building itself, which reflects all this, and, finally, everything together seen from the outside forming one spectacle, with the exhibition space becoming an exhibit and thus invisible.

It seems to me that this quality of being present but at the same time invisible is a fundamental quality, for it is this form of what could be called secret invisibility that most effectively counteracts hegemonic visibility, that dictatorship of the transparent in which everything must be visible and legible and where the problem is to invest mental and visual space, which is no longer a space for seeing but a space to be seen.

This assumes an architecture capable of creating both place and non place and of maintaining the prestige of the transparent without exercising its dictatorship, which results in unidentified, unidentifiable objects that challenge the surrounding order and have a dual, conflicting relationship with the real order. It is in this sense that we can speak not of their truth but of their radicality. If this duel does not occur, if architecture has to be the functional, programmatic transcription of constraints posed by the social and urban order then it no longer exists as architecture. A successful object is one that has an existence beyond its own reality, that creates for the public a dual relationship (not just an interactive one) consisting of misappropriation, contradiction and destabilisation.

The problem is the same in the fields of philosophy and writing, and in the political and social order. In all of them, whatever one does one cannot choose an event; one can choose only the concept. But that remains. The concept inevitably enters into conflict with the context, with all the positive, functional meanings that a building or a theory or indeed anything else can assume. The concept is something that in relation to the event as it presents itself, as it is interpreted or over-interpreted by the media and the news, creates a non-event. It sets a theoretical and fictional non-event against a so-called real event.

Naturally I understand better how this happens in writing. I see it less well for architecture but in the case of certain objects I feel this kind of illusion, of extrapolation, of another space, another setting, as an aspiration required by each project and each functional constraint. I think it is the only solution to the impossible exchange of space and city, a solution that is obviously not to be found in the artificial spaces that have been created.

This brings us to the question of the destiny of architecture when it lays claim to certain truths. What happens to the search for truth, that is to the determined ambition to fulfil a programme, to meet social and political needs, to transform social data with a cultural, pedagogic mission, etc.; in short, to all those things that feed official discourse and that relate to the conscious will of the architect himself? Fortunately or unfortunately, what we see is that the goals of the programmes are always misappropriated by those for whom they were intended, that is by the user, by that mass of people whose original or perverse response can never be written into the project. There is no automatic writing of social relations or mass needs, either in politics or architecture. Here, too, there is always a duel and the reaction is unpredictable. It is the reaction of a major player whom there is often a tendency to include as a passive element but who does not necessarily obey the rules of the game or the laws of dialogue. The masses take over the architectural object in their own way and even if the architect himself has not been diverted from his programme, the object will be diverted in any case, for its users will ensure that they restore to it the unpredictable destiny that it lacked. This, too, is a form of radicality albeit an involuntary one.

In this way all the intentions behind the Pompidou Centre have been thwarted by the object itself. A project that was based on positive perspectives – culture, communication – in the end succumbed to the reality – the hyperreality – of the object itself. Massive usage contradicted all the human and cultural aims of the project. Instead of being contextual it has created a void around it. Its flexible, scattered spaces, its transparency that was supposed to be in tune with modern man, came face to face with the masses who rendered it opaque and abused it in their own way. Contradiction has thus played the wild card and for the Pompidou has provided a sort of destiny.

The object, the true object, carries within it a certain fatality from which doubtless one should not attempt to escape. This calls into question the control of the creator, as it should. Just when he is tempted to add his signature to a function and a place, that is to fill a space according to a fixed plan, the other, all the others, will ensure that they make it a non-place and empty it of all meaning, by inventing new rules. This is in a way immoral but, as we know, it is neither morality nor a positive value system that enables a society to advance, but rather immorality and vice. There must exist in the imaginary as well as in space an ineluctable curve that runs counter to any planning, reality, or programming. In such circumstances the architect himself can play at thwarting his own plans but he cannot claim to control the object as an event, the symbolic rule being that the player must never be greater than the game itself. We are all players. That is to say that what we hope for most intensely is that from time to time rational links will unravel and for just a brief moment be replaced by an unexpected sequence of a different order, a wonderful outstripping of events, an extraordinary, predestined succession where one has the impression that things, until then maintained artificially apart, are suddenly no longer random but converge and run together spontaneously at the same intensity because they are interconnected. Our world would be unlivable without this power of divergence, without this radicality from elsewhere, from the object not the subject, and without this strange attraction.

I think that architects themselves find it seductive to imagine that the buildings that they build, the spaces they invent, are places that are secret, random, unpredictable, poetic in a way, and not just official places resulting from sociologists' statistics. That said, we are now confronted in our contemporary world – and this is valid in all fields not only architecture – by a quite different dimension, a dimension where the question of truth and of radicality is not even posed because we have crossed over into the realm of virtuality. And here there is a major risk, which is that architecture no longer exists at all, that there is no more of it. There are different ways for architecture not to exist. Man conceived and built his environment according to spontaneous rules and this inhabited space was not made for contemplation. It had no aesthetic value. Even today what pleases me in certain American cities is that architecture has been forgotten. One can travel through them without ever thinking about architecture. One can move around in them as in a desert without the make-believe of art, of the history of art, of aesthetics, of architecture. These cities permit a return to a primitive form of space. They are, of course, structured for multiple purposes but, as they are, they are like a pure event, a pure object, and not that pretence of architecture that sets itself on a pedestal. In this sense it is architecture that plays the role of anti architecture. What is more, Rem Koolhaas's famous book *Delirious New York* reveals how Manhattan was built on the basis of something that had nothing architectural about it, the Coney Island amusement park. For me that is perfect architecture which by its dimensions removes any trace of itself and where space represents thought itself. This is valid for art also, and for painting. There is no stronger work than one that has no pretension to be art, history of art, aesthetics. And it is the same thing for thought. There is no thought stronger than that which no longer has pretensions of profundity or the history of ideas or truth.

But with the virtual we are no longer dealing with architecture that knows how to play on the visible and the invisible and to keep a secret, with architecture as symbolic form playing simultaneously with mass and gravity and their disappearance. It is architecture that no longer has any secrets at all, that has become a simple operator of visibility, screen architecture, and to some extent instead of being the natural intelligence of space and city it has become their artificial intelligence. I have nothing against artificial intelligence except when it claims in its universal calculation to absorb all other forms and to reduce mental space to numeric space. To evaluate this risk, which is also the risk that the adventure of architecture will end, I shall take an example from another field with which I am more familiar, that of photography. According to Wilhelm Flusser's hypothesis the great majority of photographic images today represent neither a choice nor a vision of the subject of the image but a simple extension of the technical virtuality of the camera. It is the machine that is in control, that seeks out all the possibilities. Man is merely the technician of the programme. That is the meaning of virtual. It uses up all the technical virtualities of the camera. This analysis can be extended to the computer and to artificial intelligence where in most cases thought is merely a combination of logistics, the virtual and infinite working of the machine. And so everything that results from technique and the immense possibilities for diversification it provides leads to an automatic representation of the world. And this is also true of architecture when it is exposed to all the technical possibilities. And I do not mean only materials and construction techniques but also form. Just as all images are possible with a camera – which makes no demands except to function – so all architectural forms can be brought up to date from a virtual stock whether in or out of order. The result is that architecture no longer refers back to some truth, to some originality, but merely to the availability of techniques, forms and materials. The truth manifested is no longer that of objective conditions and even less that of the subjective will of the architect but simply that of the machine, of its technical possibilities and its operation. We may still choose to call this architecture but it is not certain that that is what it is. Let us take, for example, the Guggenheim Museum in Bilbao, the virtual object *par excellence*, the prototype of virtual architecture designed on computer using elements or combinative modules, just as a thousand similar museums could be built by a simple change of software or calculation tables. Its relation to its contents – the collection and works of art – is totally virtual. It symbolises only the performance and the setting of applied mental working or technology – not just any old one I admit – and the object itself is miraculous but it is an experimental miracle on a par with the biogenetic exploration taking place elsewhere; and it, too, will lead to a multitude of clones and chimeras. The Guggenheim is a spatial chimera, the fruit of intrigues that have taken over from architectural form itself. It is in fact a "ready made." Technology and equipment are turning everything into "ready mades." All the elements that will be combined are there at the outset and they need only a stage, like most post-modern forms. Duchamps did it with his bottle stand, with a real object that he turned into a virtual object simply by moving it. Today we do this with computer sequences and programmes, but it is the same thing. We take them as they are and put them in an architectural setting where they eventually become works of art. And on the subject of art we can ask ourselves, what is this "acting out" of Duchamps that consists of transposing any object into the sphere of art simply by moving it, an aesthetic moving that puts an end to aesthetics but which leads to an aesthetic generalization? This revolution of the "ready made," which consists in taking real objects, the real world, as a programme set in advance for an automatic aesthetic operation and which provides an infinite perspective since all objects can enter into this virtual performance – does this radical intervention that occurred in the field of art and painting have its equivalent in architecture? Is there the same sort of break in the history of architecture, a sudden implosion, a brutal event in the sublime meaning of aesthetics with the result that everything that happened from then on in the field of art no longer had the same meaning? All that occurs, to some extent, beyond the end, on the basis of the disappearance of art as such. And I should like to ask the same question with regard to architecture. Is there something that has occurred in the history of architecture that has had the result that everything that has occurred since has done so on the basis of the disappearance of architecture as such; I mean as history, as configuration, as the symbolic configuration of society. I find this an attractive hypothesis and, as something beyond their discipline, it should seduce even architects.

This question can be asked in politics also. Doesn't all that occurs on the so-called political scene occur on the basis of the disappearance of politics and the political will as such? This can be summed up as a more general hypothesis: does everything that occurs today in any field take place on the basis of the disappearance of the real and in the realm of the virtual? This hypothesis is not without hope. Perhaps it is much more interesting to see what happens beyond the end rather than purely and simply prolonging the history of art. It makes all that happens after this disappearance both original and exceptional. Everything can appear again, provided there is a hypothesis of disappearance. I like the radicality of this hypothesis because I should like architecture, the architectural object, to remain something exceptional and not be corrupted by all that lies in wait for us today on all sides in the virtual reality of architecture. And we are there. Architecture today is devoted to a great extent to culture, to communication, that is to the virtual aestheticization of the whole of society. It serves as a museum for the conditioning of that social form called culture, of immaterial needs that have no definition other than their inscription in innumerable cultural buildings. When people are not made into museum pieces where they stand in museums, where they become the virtual actors of their own life, a kind of living "ready mades" transformed into fossils, they are set down in or drawn towards the vast more or less interactive warehouses that are the commercial cultural centres of the whole world, or towards places of circulation and transit, virtual spaces so rightly dubbed "vanishing places." In Osaka, in Japan, a memorial to twenty-first century communication has already been built.

Today architecture is the slave of these functions of circulation, information, communication and culture. There is here a gigantic functionalism that is no longer of a mechanical world, a world of organic needs, of real social relations, but a functionalism of the virtual, which is most often attached to useless function where architecture itself risks becoming a useless function. The risk is the proliferation throughout the world of an architecture of clones and more or less identical cloned buildings that are transparent, interactive, mobile, ludic, in the image of virtual networks and virtual reality, in which all of society devotes itself to the comedy of culture, the comedy of communication, the comedy of the virtual, just as it devotes itself to the comedy of politics and finally to the comedy of art and architecture.

Can there be an architecture of real time, an architecture of flux and networks, an architecture of absolute or virtual visibility, of what is operational, of transparency; a polymorphic architecture with a variable purpose. A delightful small museum built in Nice by Kenzo Tange remained empty for several years with no contents but it could be perceived as a museum of the void. It could just as easily have become a craft centre or anything else. Most of today's collective buildings are too large and give an impression of emptiness rather than of space; and the works and the people that circulate there are themselves like virtual objects. There seems to be no necessity for their presence, a sort of empty functionality, a functionality of useless space. I am thinking especially of the Centro Cultural de Belém in Lisbon, France's Grande Bibliothèque, etc.

Today everything is caught up in this metastasis of culture, which is not that of architecture. It is very difficult today to distinguish what is secret in a building – that individuality I spoke of and which I do not think has really disappeared for I believe it to be indestructible – from what has been devoured by culture, a culture embracing all existing technologies and which is itself a mental technology influenced by every available model. Obviously, the architect is subject to urban and geographical constraints, the constraints of the commission, financial constraints, but there are above all models, those in the head of the developer or the client but also those that circulate in the architectural journals and that are part of the history of architectural forms. All these models impose a certain number of parameters, which means that very often the result is a collage of objects that constitutes the compromise that will pose the least problems. The drama of contemporary architecture is this endless cloning of the same type of housing all over the world based on the parameters of functionality or on the pretext of remaining faithful to a culture in terms of typical or picturesque architecture, the final result being an architectural object that not only fails to go beyond its own project but no longer goes beyond its own programme.

Has architecture lost its shadow like Chamasse's hero Peter Schlemihl who sold his name to the devil? Once it has become transparent to all available models, it will do nothing but repeat itself ad infinitum, or model itself on all the nuances of a programmed code, the sort of code that declines its generic stock of conventional forms just like a genetic code.

Looking again at the twin towers of the World Trade Center, I do not deny the architectural event that it constitutes and that I find admirable. It can be said that one is the shadow of the other, the exact replica. But, in fact, the shadow is no longer there; it has become a clone. The role of otherness, of secrecy and mystery of which the shadow is the metaphor has disappeared leaving a genetic copy of the same, where the loss of the shadow signifies the disappearance of the sun, without which, as we know, things would not be what they are. And, effectively, in our virtual universe, our universe of clones, our universe without shadows, things are only what they are. And they are what they are in innumerable copies, multiplying freely, for to some extent the shadow is the measure of the being, it sets its limits and is what prevents it from reproducing itself ad infinitum.

But all hope is not lost. Even if architecture is no longer the invention of a world, we can hope that it is something more than the invention of its more or less kitsch or designer self, something more than a geological layer of concrete, a new sedimentation of the quaternary that covers the whole planet.

The field of photography offers the possibility of wresting some exceptional images by bypassing the automatic use of the camera, which has infinite technical potential and a tendency to engender a flow of uncontrollable images. As we know, automatic writing is never truly automatic and there is always the chance of a material accident or an unforeseen sequence. In the visual profusion of images that overwhelm us there is still the chance of recreating the original, primitive setting of the image. In a certain sense, all images retain something of the wild and fantastic, and our intuition can find this punctum (to use Barthes' word), this secret of the image, provided that we take it literally. But it is up to us to want such literalness. It is up to us to make secret this secret, to ensure the failure of the general aestheticization and the mental technology of culture. And so it is conceivable that in architecture too we can start from the genius loci, from the pleasure of the place, while taking into account things that are often in the realm of change, to invent other strategies and other settings; to work against the universal cloning of human beings, of places, of buildings and against the irruption of a universal reality, what I shall call a poetic

> There is here a gigantic functionalism…of the virtual, that is most often attached to useless function where architecture itself risks becoming a useless function

transfer of situation or a poetic situation of transfer. Towards a poetic architecture, a dramatic architecture, a literal architecture, a radical architecture, of which, of course, we all dream. No truth, no aesthetic value, nothing based on the function, the meaning, the project or the programme but everything in its literalness. One more example. The Pompidou Centre again. What is the origin of the Pompidou? Does it speak of art, of aesthetics, of culture? No. It speaks of circulation, of stocks, of flows of individuals, objects and signs. And the architecture of the Pompidou states this very clearly. Literally, it is an object born out of an obscure disaster. More precisely, from the obscure disaster of culture. What is fantastic, even if it is involuntary, is that it reveals both culture itself, and to what it has succumbed. What it is succumbing to more and more is perfusion, suffusion, to the confusion of all signs. This is also true of the World Trade Center. The miracle is that it provides a fantastic spectacle of the city, of verticality at its most radical, and is at the same time a flagrant model of what the city is succumbing to; it is the symbol of what the city died of as a historical form. What makes this architecture so powerful is that it is at the same time a form of extreme anticipation and retrospective nostalgia for a lost object.

These were a few fragments on architecture as seen through the imagination of an outsider. You can interpret them literally and in every sense, as Rimbaud put it, one of the possible meanings being that there still exists beyond all illusion or disillusion a future for architecture in which I believe, even if that future of architecture is not necessarily architectural.

There is a future for architecture for the simple reason that we have not yet invented the building, the architectural object that will put an end to all the rest, to space itself; nor have we invented the city that will put an end to all cities, nor the thought that will put an end to all thought. That is our fundamental dream. But until it is achieved, there is still hope.

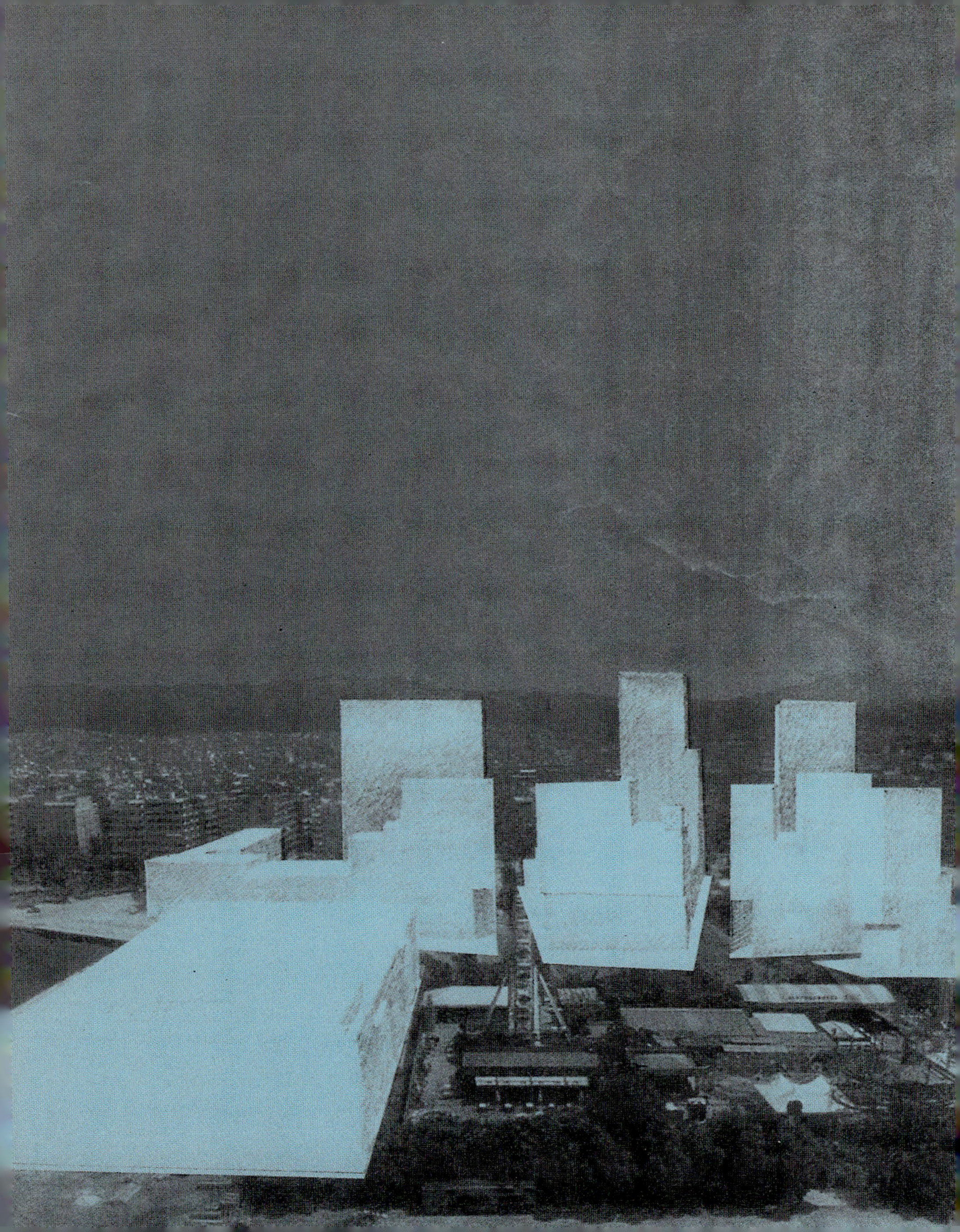

◀ Waterfront – Cityfront, Thessaloniki

IGNASÍ DE SOLÀ MORALES

Present and Futures

When in London, New York, Istanbul or Barcelona we close our eyes to most of their buildings, while guide books show us exquisite objects, old buildings and districts, as if these were the true essence of these cities and their architecture

New Architecture 5: *Truth, Radicality and Beyond in Contemporary Architecture*, 2000

"Now is tomorrow," says a line from a poem by the Catalan poet Miquel Martí i Pol. Architectural culture has for too long been living in nostalgia. Architects speak of architecture of the past: of the recent past or of a thousand years ago. The progressive transformation of culture into a museum piece has led to a view dominated by the values of what history has established as a heritage that weighs upon the present.

The crisis of modernity has generated a blockage to viewing the future with anything but a blinding admiration for the great landmarks of architectural history.

The peripheries of all the big cities have grown spectacularly in the last thirty years as the fruit of an urban revolution, the significance of which has no precedent in the history of humanity.

The situation we have reached is one of genuine schizophrenia in architectural culture: on the one hand, nostalgia for the past; on the other, the uneasy conscience of the present.

Furthermore, there is no discourse to explain and assume the magnitude of what is actually happening. What is needed, immediately, is a new "Rappel à Messieurs les architectes" like Le Corbusier's famous call to order in *Vers une architecture*.

To eyes that do not see, there is no point in showing what the engineers are doing, as they did in the 1920s, but what we ourselves are doing, what architecture is doing to respond to the imperious demands of new needs and extensions, new colonisations, new technologies. When in London, New York, Istanbul or Barcelona we close our eyes to most of their buildings, while guide books show us exquisite objects, old buildings and districts, as if these were the true essence of these cities and their architecture.

We spend most of our life in office and business centres, on sports fields, at airports and metro stations, in peripheral homes and shopping centres. However, such architecture seems banal, often sad; it lacks the quality that we believe we find in the city and in traditional architecture.

In fact, though, things may seem not to be thus. We have not yet learned to dominate movement, telematisation, provisional qualities and extension. We have no clear replies to the phenomena of building in constant change, accumulation, the disassociation between the need to create a rhetorical place and to contribute to public spaces where interaction does not become unbearable.

These are the problems we should examine, not only from the viewpoint of city planning but also – and more especially – from that of constructing architecture.

Paper contributed to the Hydra Symposium, 1995, in honour of Dimitri Fatouros

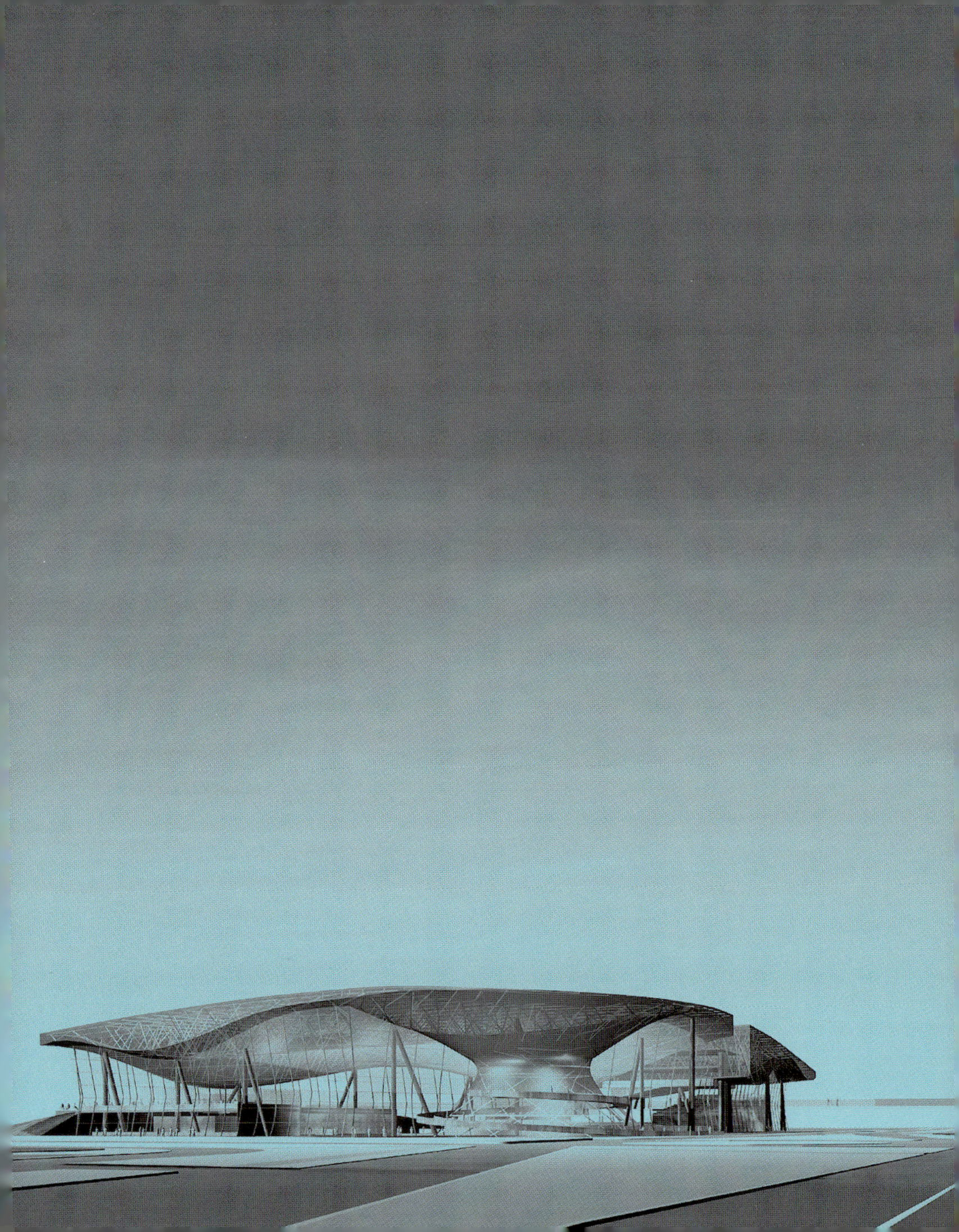

◀ BMW Welt, Munich – perspective

WOLF PRIX

In Between or Only Unstable Points can be Points of Departure

A guy who at the airport finds at the right time the right plane to take him to the right place, compared to a nomad who finds the tracks through the desert by the stars, is a non-complex-thinking, one-dimensional guy

The other day I read a book about architecture which divided the architecture of today into two schools: the hi-tech school; and the "building boxes" school. But I would call the high-tech guys "nineteenth-century engineers," and the box-builders the "prophets of obedience."

It is too simple to divide architecture into two schools. There must be a third way of thinking. And to describe this third way, I would like to quote one of your countrymen: Che Guevara. He said – and this is the point – "Be realistic. Think the impossible." The book I read said that so-called deconstructivist architecture is over, because dynamic shapes and forms have gone out of fashion. I think the author confused many things: first of all he is confused about what is dynamic. Then he has confused deconstructivist architecture with architecture *in toto*. I think there is a misunderstanding that must be clarified because they call us deconstructivists and blame us for crazy forms, but the deconstructivist method of thinking is related to Jacques Derrida's method of analytic thinking and analyzing text in order to question the rational way of thinking in Europe. That is deconstructivist architecture – an architecture that questions the rationality of life in Europe today.

Be realistic. Think the impossible
Ernesto Che Guevara.

I should like to define some paradigms at the forefront of our work in the last couple of years. If you asked me how I would define architecture I would say that architecture does not complete function but is rather the improvement of the illusion of reality. The eye is the most powerful organ to perceive architecture but it is not the only organ. To experience space you have to use your body as well. It means you can read the cross section or the plan but in order to experience it you have to walk through it. The eye, and mistrusting the eye, the brain. There is research from MIT which suggests that, unlike analogue images, digitized images do not enter the long-term memory but only the short-term memory and I think this will be revolutionary in the next few years. You have to imagine that if you draw only on the computer and if you see movies only in digitized form, you can go to the same movie two weeks later and you will see it as a new work.

A German writer has defined upcoming society by comparing a nomad with contemporary man. He says that a guy who at the airport finds at the right time the right plane to take him to the right place, compared to a nomad who finds the tracks through the desert by the stars is a non-complex-thinking, one-dimensional guy. What does this mean? I think we are going towards a more and more complex society, which means that for architecture complex solutions do not have simple answers. Six thousand years ago mankind decided which way he had to go, namely, the change from a matriarchal system into patriarchal societies. And you can read that in city plans.

When people describe our architecture they always say it is disquieting and chaotic. So what is the opposite of disquieting and chaotic? It is, of course, law and order. A polemic against simplifying architecture too much is that a chicken has to learn two images in order to survive feeding in a meadow: it can stay if it sees a goose but it has to run if it sees a falcon. The astonishing thing is that the chicken does not have to see the complex movement of the bird. It runs if it sees one abstraction and it stays if it sees another abstraction. This means that if you reduce your thinking too much there is a danger that you will share the point of view of a chicken.

We have to triple the risk in order to make architecture

But what can we say about the future of architecture? There are a lot of theories about how architecture should be explained in the future. We have another theory, one more theory. What we want to do is to finish the Tower of Babel. The Tower of Babel was prevented from being completed by an authority that brought the confusion of language to our society. We think that we have to confuse our language again in order to acquire the variety and complexity needed to complete the Tower of Babel.

Actually the title of this lecture should be that only unstable points can be points of departure. And looking for unstable points and points of departure that describe the network of a rigid system has been at the forefront of our work for perhaps the past ten or fifteen years. And we try to find it by looking at the ground plan in the same way that we look at the cross section, which means that the cross section and the ground plan are equal to each other and in between there is space which is, of course, liquid. We try to define the point of departure by finding the unstable points and trying to define the liquid spaces as well. We did this step by step in our winning entry for Moulins Sénart and it led to a master plan but the most interesting thing is that we defined the unstable points by supporting the weaker parts. In this case the low density structures were stronger than the high density structures meaning that in a short time these points were very valuable on many levels. Actually, it became not a two-dimensional but a three-dimensional master plan although it is not, of course, a proposal for buildings.

> When people describe our architecture they always say it is disquieting and chaotic. So what is the opposite of disquieting and chaotic? It is, of course, law and order

And there is another code in the Moulins Sénart project. The code of getting back public spaces. In Europe we are in danger of losing public spaces because the cities are broke: they have to sell the ground and the land to investors, and developers are doing what they have to do: they have to squeeze money out of every square metre, which means that they create only monofunctional, capitalistic structures. We architects have to gain public space by inventing strategies and one of these strategies is that we propose in this case that every 50m there must be an area for free public use.

It was fifteen years ago now that we were able to realize one of these ideas, namely the idea of public space in the middle of a building. In a social housing project in Vienna, an eighteen metre high-rise, mid-rise, and in between these two zones where the normal building goes into the high rise codes and rules there is a free zone which people can use as they wish. There are other issues as well. The slanted shapes of the leaning towers define the urban space in a very specific way and the façades support the climate. The typology of the high rise is inverted so that each floor is different. Free space in the middle of a high rise is open to every inhabitant and it is, of course, the idea of a vertical city.

For the cinema complex in Dresden we had to define an urban area and we did it by exchanging the axial thinking by tensions and vectors and thus made room in an area connected to an existing cinema for the new cinema which was to house auditoriums with 3000 seats. By studying the dynamic of the city plan and the dynamic of the people flow, and overlaying it, a certain kind of model came out which is not only defined by concrete, but also by light, in a reference to the movies. Light as a building material can only be used when it's dark. So if you look at cities in the daytime and at night-time, they are very, very different. And so these are the two levels we played on. The space sequences are reduced to a building, a building which consists of two parts: the block where the cinemas are organized and the lobby. Usually, the lobby is only the box office where you can buy tickets. But here we made an urban balcony out of this simple lobby in order to get the point of departure for the development in the city of Dresden. If you look at the city plan the new cinema is at a strategic point. It's close to the old part of the city; it's new because it was terribly bombed in the Second World War and rebuilt in the idea of a misunderstood Modernist architecture. There are a lot of slabs and actually the new ideas for city planning are not so far from what exists here. We connected the cinema block visually to the existing cinema and we made the cinema a point of departure on the one hand and the possibility for a passage on the other hand. This means that this building is a transitorial building. You can walk through it to go to the cinemas but you can also cross through it. The area is low density now but, because of the cinema, there will be an increasing density.

The other thing was the typology. The typology of the cinema complex reads like that in every city. The auditoriums are stabled one above the other and in front there is a kind of glass lobby. What we did in order to get more freedom and in order to provide the passage from one street to the other was to introduce the concept of cantilevering. This shows the typology of the building. It's more than just a volume: it's like a theatre, an introduction to the movies on the one hand and the passage on the other. If you go to your client and say that you want to build a building that is cantilevered, normally he will fire you because everyone knows that cantilevering is much more expensive than building a straightforward block, a box. But we could prove in this case that if the client would cantilever the whole building in order to get a passage through the building he would have to buy less land than if it were a block as he would only have to pay for the air rights of the building and the expenses of the cantilevering were equal to the expenses of buying the land.

There was another issue. How could we use this crystal-like building for more than just box offices? How could we manoeuvre within the volume to show that the time of central perspective is over. I believe that central perspectives are obsolete now that man has conquered outer space where there is no gravity and people can roll around their own body.

Introducing sculptures in space on the one hand defines the space and on the other creates a kind of built video clip. People walking through, experience a very different image from each point of view.

Studying how this could work led back to a project we did three years ago, a project for a kind of museum of knowledge in Kyoto where we carved out a volume which is the reading area and placed the shape right in front of the building, like a sculpture in space defining the space at one end and informing people that something is happening in the block.

The other issue, as you will see later, is dissolving the façade from the building. In a research building in Austria we glazed the façade that controls light and thus climate in the building. We placed it in front of the building and dissolved it from the building so that we created an in-between space with no function that people can use as they wish.

Back to the sculptures in space at the cinema in Dresden. They are a kind of enlargement of the concrete block because the columns are concrete. On the other hand, using metal in this way increases the crystal which is constructed of metal and glass. So there are two movements in this space showing that there is a transition action.

The sculptures in space move out from the concrete block; the pillars are concrete and the others are metal moving into the concrete blocks. There are two movements. Then we use the kind of light concept that is different in summer and in winter and in the daytime and the evening because it changes from warm light from the floor to cold light from the top and there are different shades according to the time of year as well. When people asked us years ago what our role models in architecture were, we always answered the Rolling Stones, especially Richard playing guitar solo in *Gimme Shelter*. It is exactly the same tension that we want to give. It was kind of true.

The finished cinema looks different from every side. We call it the Janus-headed concept. At least two points of views, two views. If you walk around you can read it from every side and it is very different. The façade we placed on the concrete is a metal gridded façade on one side and it is fascinating because when the light is right and the sun is shining and hitting this façade it sometimes looks like liquid glass. And this is what we would call liquid space: it defines the urban space but it doesn't close it. It is exactly 40m high and you have to walk up in order to go to the cinemas; there are a lot of stairs and a lot of ramps and bridges. One bridge leads nowhere – we call it the architects' bridge; it is the architects' bridge because we were standing up there looking down when the building was opened.

The cinemas are placed 12m and 16m high and there is no escalator because we saved the money in order to make the lobby bigger. Of course there is an elevator for the disabled. People use this as a built video clip, stomping around and playing at being actors, using the stairs for performances.

The cinema changes dramatically when it's getting dark so it's really two buildings: one in daylight, another at night. The crystal is not a glowing crystal, and it is not the perfect way to describe it because a crystal is symmetrical and this is not a symmetrical building but what we are doing is investigating liquid space in an urban project.

There are two stories I would like to tell you before I close. The first is that Rem tells us that architects are always hostages who say, "We are fine," when they are asked how they are doing with a pistol to their head. I like this story very much but I like Cimino's story in his movie *The Deer Hunter* much better. It is a story about the Viet Cong and the Vietnam war. Two friends, Robert de Niro and Christopher Walken are caught by the Viet Cong and they have to play Russian roulette. Robert de Niro starts, everything went well and he says, "Give me a second bullet." His friend almost has a nervous breakdown and says, "Try it. Do it." And he did it and it went well again. So he asked for a third bullet. When he got the third bullet he shot through the three guards and they escaped. So I think we have to triple the risk in order to make architecture. I started with a quote from your countryman Che Guevara and I would like to conclude with a quote from him: "*Venceremos!*"

Article based on lectures given at the Buenos Aires Bienal, 1999

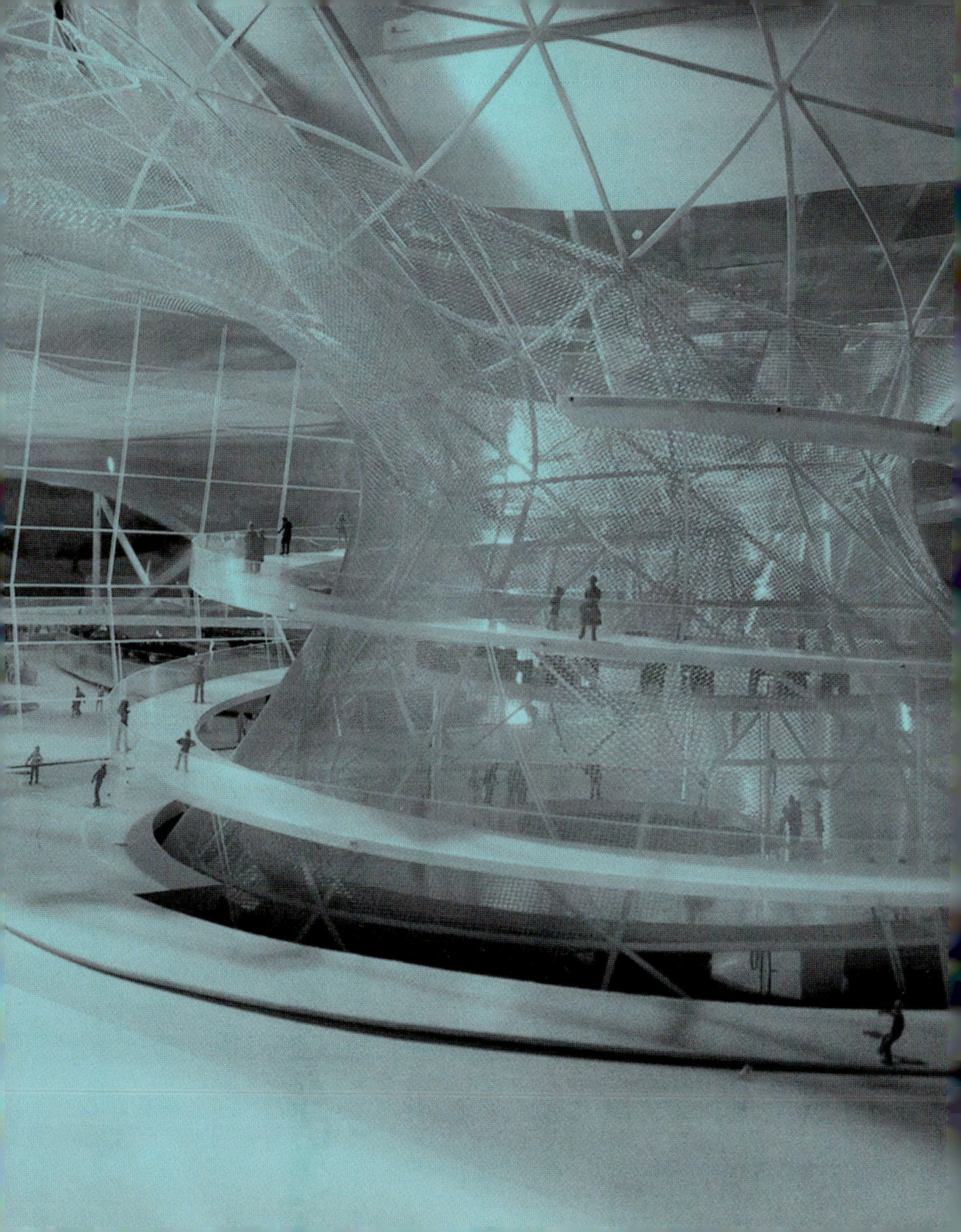

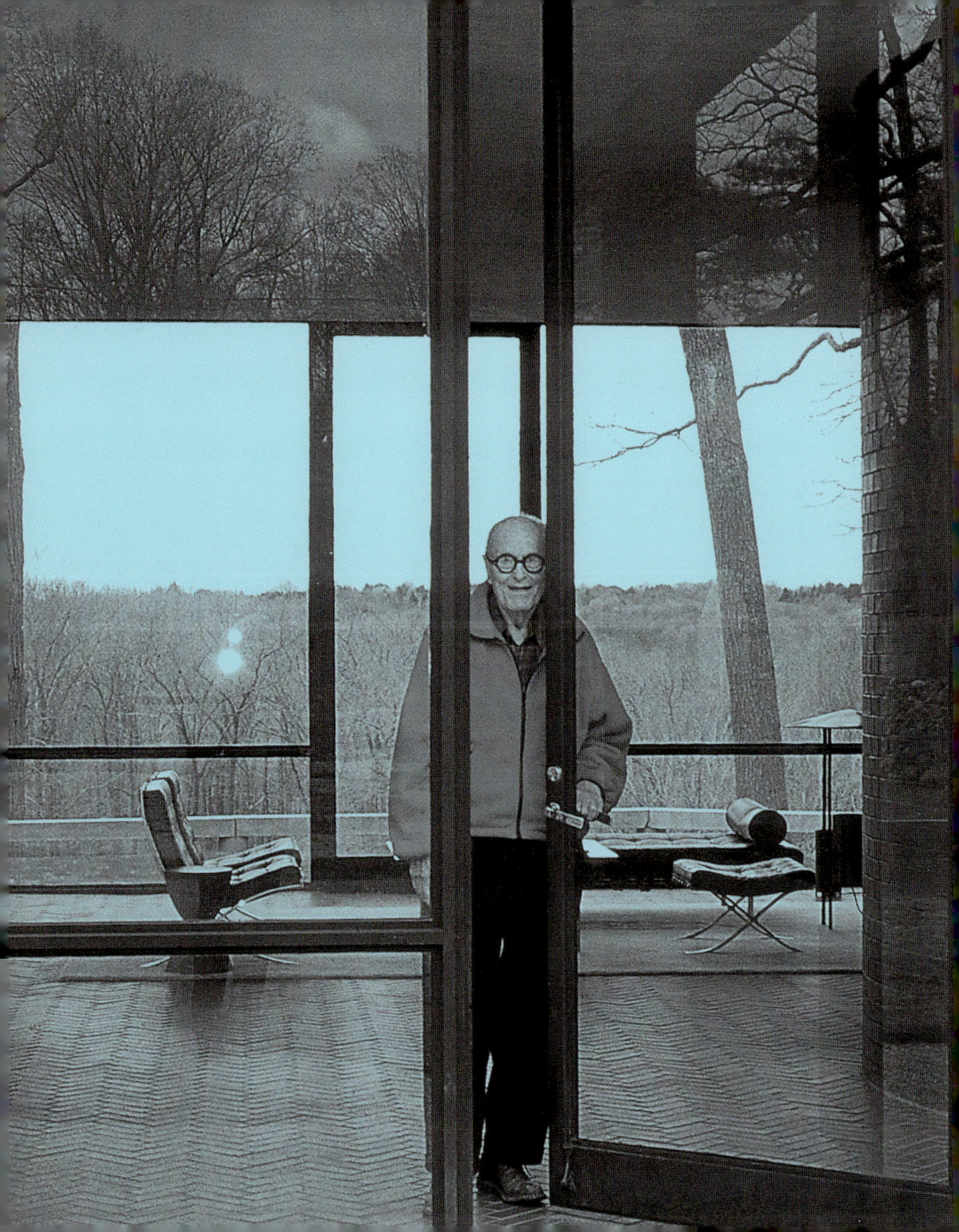

◄ Philip Johnson at the Glass House. Photo: Alexandra Papadakis

DIMITRI FATOUROS

Philip Johnson's Cathedral of Hope

*A work of architecture is always non-finite;
it is part of the process that brings a multilevel,
multilateral richness to human situations.
This Cathedral is not merely part of this trend
but a dramatic step forward*

New Architecture 5: *Truth, Radicality and Beyond in Contemporary Architecture*, 2000

The Cathedral of Hope in Dallas, Texas is a cathedral for a predominantly gay congregation. It is to replace an existing church, which the community has outgrown. The design redefines the stereotype in such a way that it is concealed: the liturgical processes are transferred and transformed into a built situation based on aspects of modernism with echoes of Louis Kahn. The design concept is a "translation" of buttresses and on folding and unfolding. In medieval buildings buttresses were the result of constructional constraints but their rich play of shadows and hidden connotations make for good design today. Johnson uses them as a means of transformation and as a symbolic geometry for the exterior and for the interior void, which he reorganizes and transforms into a spatial cosmos of his own. There is continuity throughout, resonant of the low voice of diachronicity. The internal differentiations enhance the feeling of space, organize various spatial situations, and recall a multiplicity of spatio-visual events.

There is a studied asymmetry. The entrance elements, the arrangement of the seats and the micro visual field surrounding them all differentiate the symmetries. The axis deviates from the conventional; there is a door on one side; but the expected door on the other side is not there. The wall near the staircases picks up the small wall in the background.

The portico (stoa) is an important element of a cathedral. Here it has been transformed from its origins to become almost a contradiction of the raison d'être of a portico. Johnson's design uses the type in a way that leads to a new understanding of type. This is true not only of the type. This is true of the overall scale of the work but also of the interior, where he transforms a void into space.

The non rectilinear is organized into a multi-complex erotic and sensual place. The relationships of sharp and soft, curvilinear and linear forms make it a typical expressionistic work that recalls Charoun and Mendelsohn's timid linear approach.

The shape reflects the envelope – I do not want to use the word wall since wall refers only to construction and this is not a reading of architecture based on construction methods and achievements. It is about creating space from voids. It may be an exaggeration to say that architecture is not about construction but in fact architecture uses construction but is not a translation of construction. It is the will to create space.

A work of architecture is always non finite; it is part of the process that brings a multilevel, multilateral richness to human situations. This Cathedral is not merely part of this trend but a dramatic step forward.

Philip Johnson is a master architect and a complicated one: his work is much richer than it at first appears. He modestly claims to copy his friends, referring especially to Eisenman and Gehry, but, of course, he does not but he reminds us that creative architecture does make use of the concepts of the masters and of anonymous works.

Today it is becoming more and more difficult for architecture to induce people to feel at ease, to experience sensuality, to carry on a dialogue. Neither architecture nor the arts now play an important role in the struggle against barbarism; they do not affect our well being although they may provide moments of hope, which is important on a personal level. But where does architecture stand in the battle for a less aggressive world? Even the Cathedral of Hope can only moderate the stresses faced by its congregation but it does express another way of thinking, another way of life.

XVI

◀ Plate from *Le Castel Béranger, oeuvre de Hector Guimard, Architecte*; Librairie Rouam et Cie, c.1898

PAUL GREENHALGH

The Tensile Line

The tensile line twists and pulls its way through space, toying with invisible grids of normative expectation, pulling out of the true of an underlying geometry, flouting classical system, breaking corners, defying received histories, creeping over objects as a jungle reclaims a deserted village

The most characteristic aesthetic element at work in Art Nouveau is the curving, tensile line. Commonly described as whiplash, the tensile line is one that is ready to spring into a different form, or appears to be constrained and ready to burst out. It twists and pulls its way through space, toying with invisible grids of normative expectation, pulling out of the true of an underlying geometry, flouting classical system, breaking corners, defying received histories, creeping over objects as a jungle reclaims a deserted village. It takes possession of the world of things in order to make claims for their modernity; it can become the entire structure of the thing itself, the basis of its engineering and the totality of its meaning.

It was ubiquitous. It slides out of Medusa's heads and is formed in trails of blood dripping from the Baptist's head; it snakes through the veneered landscapes and brass trimmings of a thousand buffets and wardrobes; it forms mannered forest interiors in steel and glass; it frames entrances into the underground; it drags us into the grand citadels of exchange and trade. It represented the fusion of opposites in an age of oppositions: the physical and the metaphysical, the natural and the artificial, the individual and the collective. It stood for the furious rational pace of the technological revolution while tracing the path taken by the disembodied soul in Oscar Wilde's haunting vision of love and death *The Fisherman and his Soul*.

It was the key signifier of modernity in Art Nouveau, an elegant celebration of the complexity of modernity and an all-inclusive fusion of nature, history and humanity. But the powerful directness of the tensile line gave it a simplicity that belies its meanings and origins and has led to an under-estimation of its scope. It was an eclectic invention that represented a constituency of ideas and attitudes.

Modernity remains the grand cultural debating ground of the visual arts and the struggle to define it is not simply a matter of archival neatness or the nicety of nomenclature. It affects what is accorded seriousness in the past and it will govern what is made and consumed in the future. Modernity is identified here as being a complex and multi-faceted response to material modernization. It is the recognition of the shape and flow of history, the perception that existence is premised upon movement and has the potential to be directed. Culture, in the widest anthropological sense, as well as in the more limited sense of art, does not necessarily change in immediate recognition of technical, economic or political shifts, though sometimes it does. More normally, a mixture of responses, resistances, assimilations and acceptances gives rise to complex and variegated artefacts. Modernity is not a style or a set of formulae for the construction of culture. It isn't understood simply by following colours, shapes and manifestoes back through the history of art.

Four values identify the modern sensibility: *difference; movement; responsibility*; and *self-consciousness*. Difference entails a recognition of the present as being separate and in tension with the past. We have stepped out of the flow, and no longer perceive ourselves as being in an homogeneous continuum. Movement involves the perception that existence does not so much have shape and a structure as a velocity and a potential for direction. Both can be changed and are not predetermined. Movement is a negation of stasis. The manufacturing of stasis is an inevitable result of resistance to modernization and is part of the dialectical process of modernity. Indeed, in certain circumstances modernity is entirely constituted of a resistance to modernization.

> Movement involves the perception that existence does not so much have shape and a structure as a velocity and a potential for direction...Movement is a negation of stasis

PAUL GREENHALGH

Responsibility is no more than the recognition that there is no controlling supra-force, no given, no inevitable or preordained directive. We are responsible for creating what there is. The past offers advice not a template. This is the difference between making use of history and historicism, between the invention of myth as part of material reality rather than living by myth as a non-corporeal given.

In some senses modernity is no more than its recognition of itself, the acknowledgement that while all aspects of existing culture are relative and non-linear, culture as a whole is collectively shifting away from a previous condition. This self-conscious recognition prevents culture repeating itself innocently, replicating its previous forms and ideas without an agenda. Such replication, which in the visual arts is manifested in various forms of historicism, is a conscious denial of the process of modernity and as such is part of the process of modernity.

Within the Art Nouveau camp there were various uses of nature at work and as many motivations behind these usages. For example, many designers conventionalised it by breaking it into abstracted, flattened forms for use in surface pattern. Others celebrated nature by transposing plants, animals and insects directly and realistically into their work, in a pantheistic orgy of nature worship.

While the tensile line was adopted by both conventionalisers and pantheists within the ranks of Art Nouveau, these two tendencies were not central to the driving commitment to modernity that gave the style its real meaning and shape. These can be traced to an interest in theories of evolution. Most obviously, tensile line (and a good many other forms) is clearly derived from illustrations of organic and microscopic forms in science journals, and from life studies of plant and human form. The illustrated volumes of Ernst Haeckel are the most famous of a number of works that provided designers with models. But the inspiration is only partly visual; it is also philosophical.

The tensile line was potently erotic; in stretched iron, cast concrete and carved stone, it sexualised the fabric of the city

Evolution implied a fusion of humankind with nature, a breaking down of barriers that myth and religion had kept in place for several millennia. Various Art Nouveau designers persuaded by the truth of this descent of man often made use of metamorphosis, or the fusion of the human and the non-human as a poetic ploy. At the same time, evolution gave culture a viable direction. It became synonymous with progress, the advance of humanity to a higher plane. The tensile line represents both these evolutionist visions. Its curves and springs combine sepals, stems, skin and sinews in a fusion of human and plant biology. At the same time, the line has movement and direction. Its tautness and dynamic potential for sudden growth imply a culture in movement, in process of organic shift to another condition.

It is significant that a good number of Art Nouveau designers stated their preference in their designs for stalks, stems and sepals rather than flower heads. The stalk is in constant movement upwards, it supports and underpins the condition of the whole. The sepal aids reproduction and is therefore about generational change. All these things are the functional core of the plant, its means of development and advance: the flower, on the other hand, is the static, finished, end product.

One might distinguish between designers who saw nature as *analogous* to rather than *synonymous* with modernity. The difference between analogue and synonym would have a powerful bearing on attitudes to design and society into the twentieth century. Designers who felt nature provided a model tended to feel that design decorated society and thus changed the world through a relatively straightforward improvement of the environment. The processes of nature were like those of modern life, and when translated into decoration, could decorate it to render it more tolerable. Designers tended, for example, when designing interiors, to orchestrate the disparate elements into a harmony that made the room into an artificial glade. By contrast, those who conceived of nature as synonymous with modernity understood human civilization and culture as being part of a giant, cosmic regime of advance, following evolutionist tendencies. They went beyond visual appearance into an ideologically-driven vision of nature as the site for the struggle for the human, or the place where the future could be discovered and articulated. For them nature and modernity were both processes of endless becoming, to do with the dynamic shift in the material condition of things, with movement through time and with the physical and metaphysical transformation of society. And like nature, the processes of modernity never achieve stasis. The work of designers, convinced that nature and the modern were synonymous, was ideologically directed. Interiors often conveyed a sense of organic inevitability. Through technology the city transformed the natural into the artificial, yet the city remained an organic, dynamic continuum of the natural world. Artifice is at the heart of everything sexual. The tensile line was potently erotic; in stretched iron, cast concrete and carved stone, it sexualised the fabric of the city.

Nature was not its only source. It is also saturated with obscure histories and exotic cultures, chosen for their potential to signal a sense of the other, of alternatives to the norm. The line twists and dances like the billowing silk of an exotic dancer, directly influenced by the North African and Near Eastern Islamic art arabesque forms found in script and pattern work, especially when executed on tile, carpets and silks. To European eyes, Islamic design was perfectly poised between religion and the erotic. This hedonist fusion of the spiritual and corporeal is transmitted into the tensile line.

Japan was more important than the arts of Islam. The cultural effect of Japanese culture on Europe and North America after 1860 has been accurately described in a now copious literature, none of it exaggerating the reality. Suffice it to say here that what designers found in Japan was a fully resolved alternative vision of the world, one that allowed them to escape the stultifying tedium of their training. Japanese prints, bronze statuettes and vessels, silks, sword guards, lacquer work, kimono, 'Rimpa' style scroll boxes contain linear motifs that are the single most direct source of the tensile line. These taut meanders are usually an abstraction of water, of informal activity transformed into lyrical structure.

Alongside Japan and Islam and fused with them can be found a gaggle of European past cultures. The Rococo was prominent. A beguilingly debased development of the Baroque, Rococo moved backwards and forwards in revived form between respectability and decadence from its invention in the eighteenth century to the *fin de siècle*. There is something of the loose adventure of the Rococo in the tensile line, though its florid asymmetry was never hard enough to provide the whole story. Its high sophistry could never provide the near violent energy; this came more readily from the crudity, barbarism and brutality of the Celts and Vikings and folk art. The latticed cut and thrust of the pattern work of the two ancient cultures was especially significant.

The line twists and dances like the billowing silk of an exotic dancer

Some designers created a tensile line that clearly owed a good deal to historical forebears. When affected by the Rococo, for example, the line loses much of its strength, and takes on a smoky, loose demeanour; it can be found comfortably moving around inside panelling or within the profiles of vases and figurines, rather than striving to burst out of them. It sometimes takes on the spirit of Japonisme, which owes much to eighteenth century uses of that culture. Others determined to push history so far back as to effectively eliminate any obvious reference. Invariably it was the same designers who committed themselves to an evolutionist vision of culture and society.

There was something beyond the conjoining of alternative visions of nature and culture in the tensile line. It represented, with its abrupt yet meandering tension, the new vision of the modern mind, hanging impossibly between the material and the spiritual, the natural and the sexual. It was design that lived on the edge of its nerves, that lived in the terror and speed of the new world while hankering after the mystical depth of the past. Its tenseness recognised that while absolute change is an inevitable part of the human condition, there is no certainty about the form change will take. Underneath its robustness, and in contrast with the confident fusion of evolutionism and Platonism of some of the next generation of modernists, the tensile line describes a psychic uncertainty. It represented the psychological condition of the age and described in abstract form the fretting of a generation of Symbolists.

Indeed, Art Nouveau was the single most powerful, all embracing and cumulative manifestation of the activity of Symbolists, Decadents and the Aesthetic Movement of the previous several decades. It picked up on and exploited the heritage bestowed by Gautier, Baudelaire, Verlaine, Wilde, Symons and others. It was to do with artifice, with the creation of a stylistic canon that was derived from nature without being naturalist. In rendering nature artificial for the city, and in naturalizing artifice, the designers had momentarily reconciled the opposition between nature and culture, between what is made and what grows.

The tensile line represented, with its abrupt yet meandering tension, the new vision of the modern mind, hanging impossibly between the material and the spiritual, the natural and the sexual. It was design that lived on the edge of its nerves

Art Nouveau was far from the only available vision of modern life. In fact there were strikingly anti-naturalist visions of modern humanity in the period. Karl Marx, and his immediate followers, persistently cited the *natural* as being the alienated condition. He associated nature with pre-intellectual, unconscious desires. He famously identified alienated man as being in a state whereby "the animal becomes human and the human animal." In its dogged materiality, nature for him was a condition to escape from. In the last two decades of the century, social Darwinism further negated the idea of the natural; as humankind became increasingly ranked within hierarchies, the natural became associated with the fundament of life, from which it was necessary to rise. All things sexual, feminine and primitive became associated with the natural in a damning confederation.

The need to rise above the natural toward the non-physical was also fired by a re-reading of antique philosophy. The steady revival of interest in classical idealism, and more specifically in Platonism, became central to several of the avant garde schools into the early twentieth century. The classicism of the *Section d'Or Cubists*, of *the Purists*, and especially Le Corbusier, located abstraction and functionalism as being quintessentially anti-naturalist. Animal instinct and the physical pleasures, both of which are clearly a component of Art Nouveau design, thus ultimately led to its being attacked and undermined.

Art Nouveau provided, for a short historical moment, a persuasive resolution to the problem of the issue of the position of the individual in the collective of modern life. The tensile line stood for a fusion between individual consciousness and the aspirations of society, it embodied the reconciliation of material and spiritual opposites that allowed for the creation of an all-inclusive (rather than reductive) modernism. This is because the relationship between culture and nature was resolved within the style, humanity was metamorphosed into a natural condition, fused into an emotively charged totality of design. The whiplash artifice of the tensile line held within it visions of art, technology and biology, temporarily reconciled in a visual representation of progress. It was a briefly successful attempt to generate an interdisciplinary hedonism.

As grandiose as this sentiment may be, the persistent mass popularity of Art Nouveau, despite repeated rejections of it by professional architects, designers and academics through the twentieth century, would suggest that it strikes very particular chords with very large numbers of people. Its eclecticism made it all inclusive, in a world where high culture was (and is) perceived to be exclusive.

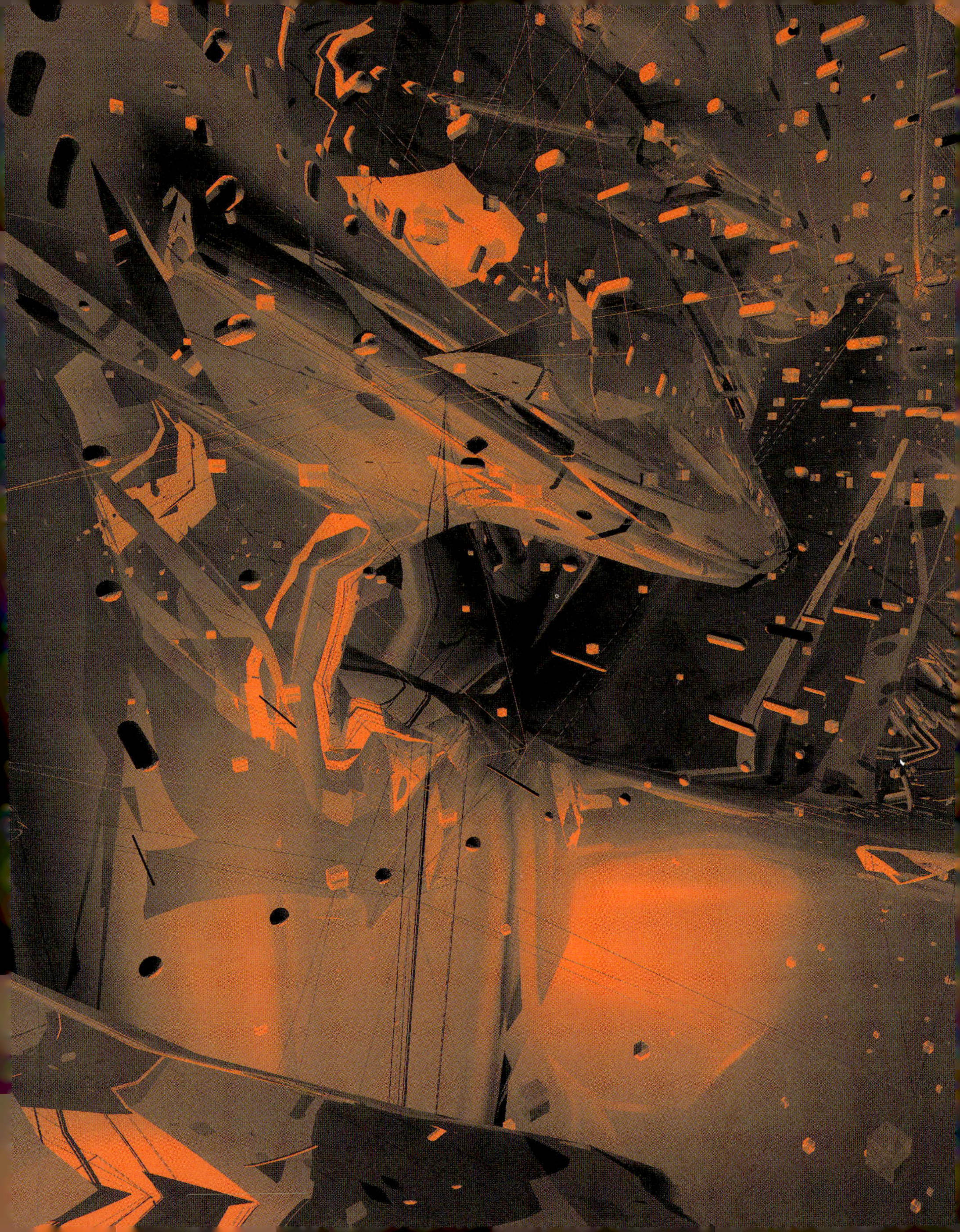

◀ *v4Dwxy* Four data-driven worlds constructed from four three-dimensional orthographic projections of a liquid four-spatial-dimensional biomathematical form

MARCOS NOVAK

Neuro~, Nano~, Bio~:
New Atomism and Living Nanotectonics

Of all the species of the invisible, the most remote is the alien; and of all the species of the alien, the most ineffable is the alien within

New Architecture 7: *Innovation – From Experimentation to Realisation*, 2003

THE VERY SMALL

"There is plenty of room at the bottom." These were the words with which physicist Richard Feynman ignited what was to become the nanotechnology revolution. In his 1959 talk at the California Institute of Technology, Feynman demonstrated the vastness of the unexplored frontier of the very small. Forty years later, armed with computational devices that already take advantage of high miniaturization, we stand at the beginning of another major technological advance: the control of the construction of the world from the grains up. In many places around the world, nanotechnology research centres have begun to build the research foundation for a wave of new industries. As the shift to the digital fades into ordinariness, computation and its corollaries become the given upon which a transition to an ever stranger, alien reality is being built.

Nanometers measure the world at the scale of a billionth of a metre, the scale of atoms and molecules, and this brings us into direct contact with a level of control over matter that approximates that of animate nature itself in many regards.

> I would like to describe a field, in which little has been done, but in which an enormous amount could be done in principle
> *Richard Feynman, 1959*

Feynman himself realised this and drew several of his examples from the biological. Nanotechnology tends to biotechnology. We cannot separate or overestimate the relation between nanotechnology and biotechnology, or that between the construction of new materials, molecule by molecule and atom by atom, and that of the mapping and inevitable alteration of the human genome, chromosome by chromosome, gene by gene, nucleotide by nucleotide, base by base.

The shift to this level of control brings with it a paradoxical loss of control. As we reach into the world of the very small, the numbers of what we want to control swell beyond our capacity to dictate order from above. The world of the very small is that world of the very many, and it requires strategies of distributed processing, assembly, and control. Like every other major technological shift, the shift to the very small requires an entirely different intellectual mode, a mode in which one must relinquish control in order to gain it; in which, even more than in the case of the algorithmic, one lets go of the submicroscopic particular – which consists of particles – in order to gain access to the macroscopic.

ABUNDANT COMPUTING

The question of the control of large numbers is not new to us – it is integral to our use of the digital. But the encounter with the very many brings up another issue: the pervasiveness of computation in nature: in quite a serious way, every particle of every grain of sand is a computer, and nature assembles itself by a computation that is ubiquitous and massively parallel. We are entering this arena of abundant computing as innocents to the lions. This is not to say that we must not enter – it is inevitable that we will; nor to say that we must be fearful – though we must be careful. It is simply to indicate how unprepared we are to think in this way, even though we do literally think this way: our consciousness itself depends on a similarly massive parallelism, constructed as it is neuron by neuron, synapse by synapse, neurotransmission by neurotransmission.

Nobel-prize laureate Gerald Edelman's theory of "neuronal group selection" shows how the genetic algorithm – Darwinism – is present in the formation of the brain, of memory, and even in the living moment of consciousness. This is the manner of operation we must capture and harness.

GROWING ARCHITECTURE

And what of Architecture? As always, there are numerous ways to draw impressionistic inspiration from the sciences of the very small, but the final challenge must surely be to once again reconceive Architecture, this time not as the built environment, but as the grown environment. New materials have always implied new architecture; nanotechnology is combining with biotechnology to create materials that are not only new, but that stand at the border of the animate and the inanimate, tending toward the living. A corresponding architecture will surely follow. These materials must be seeded, grown, and nurtured; so must the buildings that are formed by the same processes.

But there can be no mistake: as living as these buildings may be, they will also participate in the worlds that we have built before them, and specifically, in the informational matrix of cyberspace that has already escaped from the confines of computers and screens and has spilled, wirelessly, into every crevice of our cities. These living architectures will be wirelessly wired, aware as much of themselves as of every aspect of knowledge and information we choose to put on the Internet, and every inference that can be drawn from that knowledge.

ATOMIC MUSIC, ATOMIC ARCHITECTURE

Implicit in the world view of the Greek Atomists – Leucippus, Democritus, Epicurus, and in the writings of the Roman Epicurean poet Lucretius, formalized in the calculus of Newton and Leibniz, and operationalized in contemporary media by techniques such as sampling, quantization, and digital signal processing is an epistemology of the assembly of the world from the very small. Even though the limit by which we judge the very small changes, and at each new scale a different apparatus must be brought to bear on the materials we wish to organize, the fundamental insight persists and remains at the core of what we mean by knowing something about the world.

Music has already undergone the transition that architecture now faces: in going from the scale of staffs and notes to the scale of sampled bits, its entire theoretical, compositional, and performative logic had to be revised. Composers needed the conceptual and technological tools with which to order decisions at the scale of microseconds. Even before this, there was a long debate about whether sound was wavelike or "corpuscular." Following Einstein's prediction of phonons, quasi-particles consisting of wave-packets that have some of the properties of particles, Dennis Gabor described sound quanta, and composers such as Iannis Xenakis experimented with "sound clouds." Like the story of the struggle to resolve the unresolvable nature of light as wave or particle, the story of this question in sound is fascinating, and is told in detail by composer/ researcher Curtis Roads in his book *Microsound*, where he also outlines his own efforts in granular synthesis. The advent of technologies such as rapid prototyping – stereo-lithography, fused-material deposition, laminated object manufacturing – allows form to be assembled particle by particle, in much the same way as digital sound is now assembled sample by sample. Many techniques of digital sound can be brought to bear upon from controlled grain by grain but understood simultaneously as wave pattern.

N-DIMENSIONAL MODULATIONS

It is possible to organize music, image, moving image, solid, space, interaction, and liquid architectures as phenomena of increasing dimensionality. Broadly, music is one-dimensional; images are two-dimensional; solids are three-dimensional; interactive spaces are three-plus-one-dimensional (three spatial and one temporal, as opposed to four spatial), and so on. This is a partial and limited schematization, and is not meant to deny the many additional dimensions that each of these modalities carries with their many and varied attributes. Still, if we allow ourselves to consider them in this way, as instances in a continuum of modulation of ever-increasing dimensionality, we can then transpose the operations of one onto another, either by extrusion up to higher dimensions, or by projection or section down to lower dimensions.

This conception of sound, still image, moving image, still form, moving forms, still space, moving space, all as modulations of n-dimensional modalities permits us to carry the algorithmic theories and techniques of computer music into architecture. Some of this has already been done. What has not been done, and what therefore limits the transposition of compositional strategies from one to the other, is the shift in underlying representation – we have not developed a representation of architecture as streams, sheets, or clouds of bits. The techniques exist – volume rendering in scientific visualization, for instance – but they have not been adopted into the conception or execution of architecture. We understand what it means to compress a sound: but what does it mean to compress a building when that building is composed as three or more dimensional waves and built granule by granule? In music, granular synthesis is an active topic, as research and as avant-garde compositional practice. What would it mean to compose and synthesize a building grain by grain?

LIVING MUSIC, LIVING ARCHITECTURE

So far we are still in the realm of the digital. The nano~ and the bio~, to be followed by the pico~ (and, in time, the femto~, atto~, zepto~, yocto~), the quanto~, lead both architecture and music, and all the other modalities, into unexplored territories. What is nanomusic, biomusic, nanoarchitecture, bioarchitecture? The question does not seek an answer in the form of a conventionally built building that is inspired by nanotechnology or biotechnology – it seeks an answer that embodies these in its true fabric. Perhaps a nanomusical composition is a resonant nanoengineered material that, when activated, sounds a sarabande; perhaps a biomusical composition is a quasi-living sound producing organism that, when engaged, sings a symphony.

Architecture and music are synonyms for space and time; between them they address nearly everything – what remains is transactivity: mutable behaviour, evolution, life, consciousness. This is where we are headed – into a world in concord with nature but of our own making, a world within which we are transacting with artificially living, artificially conscious n-dimensional modulations of sensory and informational modalities, only vestigially, and perhaps nostalgically, named architecture or music.

PERIPHERAL EVIDENCE

The work shown here is the anticipation of these other architectures. It draws on the biological and the mathematical, the generative and the generated, the algorithmic, the genetic and the transgenic. The most intriguing direction being explored is that of creating nanoscale architectures and sculptures by using fragments of RNA as building modules.

The very small, the very large, the very fast, the very slow, the observable at the limit of observation bring the empiricism upon which science depends to the edge of epistemology. What we might have known all along is made plain: what we describe as reality is a construct based in peripheral evidence. In Leibniz's *Monadology*, reality is simply the agreement between elementary monads, a structure of coincidences exhibiting certain patterns and invariances we come to recognize and trust. If the nanoscale architecture project succeeds, how will we even know there is anything there? The architectures and sculptures produced will fit 10,000 times in the width of a human hair. A virtual reality setup will be required to design them, an algorithmic engine to sequence them, a molecular wet lab to assemble the requisite molecules and the resultant RNA architecture; rapid prototyping, interactive installations, and a host of other translations will be needed to manifest them in human scales. Each step leaves conventional architecture far behind. It is, no doubt, speculative work, work whose benefit is the formative act of constructive anticipation itself. In growing this architecture, we grow the bridge to the future.

And so, to paraphrase Feynman, I would like to describe a transvergent, living, alien architecture, in which little has been done, but in which an enormous amount could be done in principle.

Of Skin and Bone: Echinoderm_RP.
Stereolithographic model of biomathematical form based on Ernst Haeckel's studies of rediolaria. Such models can be used in three ways: a) the form itself can be replaced with living bone tissue; b) the form can be used as the substrate upon which to grow living skin; c) both of the above ▶

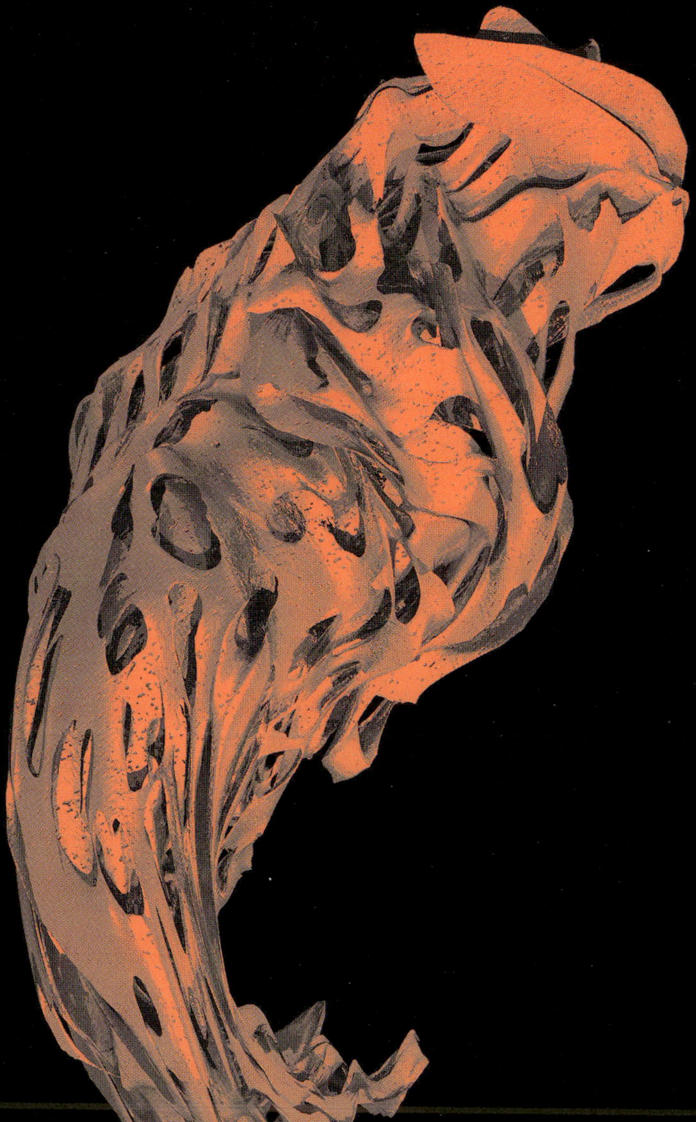

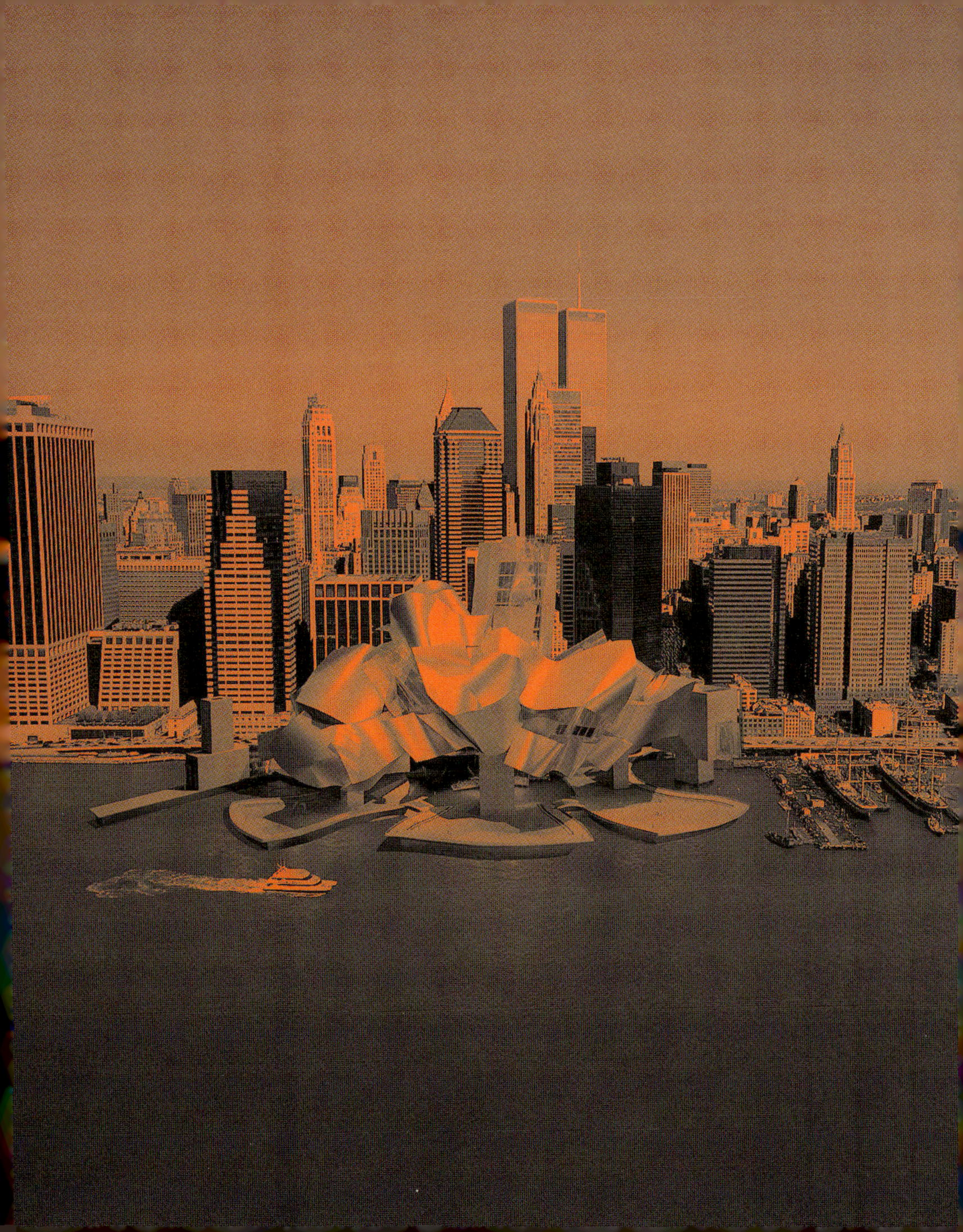

◀ Frank Gehry's proposal for the Guggenheim Manhattan. Photo Courtesy of the Guggenheim Foundation

RICHARD TAYLOR

Second Nature
Fractured Magic from Pollock to Gehry

*Given the prevalence of fractal objects in Nature,
is it possible to construct fractal buildings?
The challenge lies in the ability to repeat the
construction process at different scales*

New Architecture 7: *Innovation – From Experimentation to Realisation*, 2003

We are all familiar with the Manhattan skyline, with its many skyscrapers reaching high into the clouds. Imagine a skyscraper shaped like the clouds surrounding it. Three years ago, the Guggenheim Museum unveiled a design by Frank Gehry for a "cloud-like" building to house its modern art collection. With its swirling layers of curved surfaces spanning three piers, the proposed forty-five storey structure was predicted to reshape New York's waterfront. If it goes ahead, how will people respond to this unusual architecture? My recent studies of human reaction to fractal patterns indicate a bright future for buildings that incorporate Nature's shapes into their design.

From the first moment I saw one of Frank Gehry's buildings, his architectural style reminded me of the creations of another radical visionary – the abstract painter Jackson Pollock (1912-56). Pollock rolled vast canvases across the floor of his studio and then dripped paint directly onto them, building majestic swirling patterns. Over the last fifty years, Pollock's paintings have frequently been described as "organic," suggesting his imagery alludes to Nature. "Organic" seems an equally appropriate description for Gehry's creations. Lacking the cleanliness of artificial order, their imagery stands in sharp contrast to the straight lines, triangles, squares and wide range of other "man-made" shapes known in mathematics as Euclidean geometry. But if Pollock and Gehry's creations celebrate Nature's organic shapes, what shapes would these be? Do organic objects, such as trees and clouds, have an underlying geometry, or are they "patternless" – a disordered mess of randomness?

Jackson Pollock, *Blue Poles*:number 11. Courtesy National Gallery of Australia, Canberra

Whereas mathematicians have pursued the study of Euclidean geometry with remarkable success since its introduction in 300BC, the complexities and apparent irregularities of Nature's organic patterns in our everyday lives have proven more difficult to define. One approach, doomed to failure, was to model Nature's imagery using Euclidean shapes. "In retrospect," noted the mathematician Benoit Mandelbrot, "clouds are not spheres, mountains are not cones, coastlines are not circles, and bark is not smooth, nor does lightning travel in straight lines." The correct approach arrived in the 1970s, when Mandelbrot identified a subtle form of order lurking within the apparent disorder of Nature's scenery. Natural objects were shown to consist of patterns that recur at increasingly fine magnifications. Mandelbrot christened this repetition a "fractal" (a term derived from the Latin 'fractus', meaning fractured) to emphasise their irregular appearance when compared to the smoothness of Euclidean shapes. Catalogued in his epic work *The Fractal Geometry of Nature* (1977), a range of natural objects were shown to be fractal, including mountains, clouds, rivers and trees. Natural fractals, such as the tree shown opposite left are referred to as statistical fractals. Although the patterns observed at different magnifications are not identical, they have the same statistical qualities such as pattern density, degree of roughness, etc. This type of fractal pattern stands in contrast to exact fractals, shown opposite right, where the patterns repeat exactly at different magnifications.

Given the prevalence of fractal objects in Nature, is it possible to construct fractal buildings? The challenge lies in the ability to repeat the construction process at different scales. Exact fractals are the simpler proposal because the same shape is employed at each magnification. For this reason, exact fractals have appeared regularly throughout the history of art, dating back to Islamic and Celtic patterns. This exact repetition can be extended to three dimensions. An obvious example is that of Russian dolls. In terms of architecture, the Castel del Monte, designed and built by the Holy Roman Emperor Frederick II (1194-1250), has a basic shape of a regular octagon fortified by eight smaller octagonal towers at each corner. A more recent example is Gustave Eiffel's tower in Paris, where the repetition of a triangle generates a shape known amongst fractal geometrists as a Sierpinski Gasket. The Eiffel Tower serves as a demonstration of the practical implications of fractal architecture. If, instead of its spidery construction, the tower had been designed as a solid pyramid, it would have consumed a large amount of iron, without much added strength. Instead Eiffel exploited the structural rigidity of a triangle at many different size scales. The result is a sturdy and cost-effective design. Gothic cathedrals also exploit fractal repetition in order to deliver maximum strength with minimum mass. The fractal character also dominates the visual aesthetics of the building. A Gothic cathedral's repetition of different shapes (arches, windows and spires) on different scales yields an appealing combination of complexity and order. In contrast to the "filled-in" appearance of the Romanesque structures that pre-dated it, the carved out character of the Gothic buildings delivers a distinctive skeletal appearance that results in their remarkable luminosity. More recently, the visual appeal of Frank

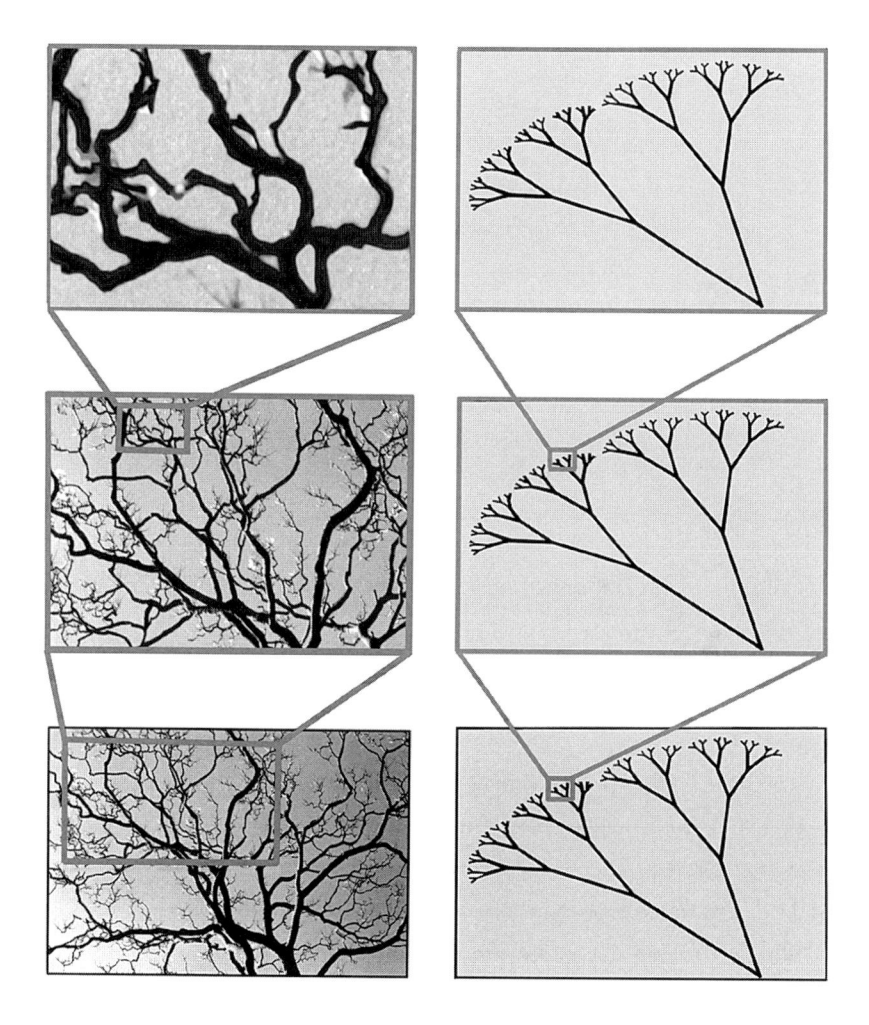

Natural fractals in the form of trees
(known as statistical fractals)

Exact fractals, where the patterns repeat
exactly at different magnifications

191

RICHARD TAYLOR

Lloyd Wright's Palmer House in Ann Arbor (USA) of 1950-51 has been analysed in terms of Lloyd's use of triangular shapes at different scales.

In contrast to the exact fractals discussed above, statistical fractals represent a far greater challenge to both artists and architects. M.C. Escher is known within the art world for his mathematical dexterity and his ability to manipulate repeating patterns at different scales. However, even Escher restricted himself to drawing exact fractals and did not attempt to capture the intricacy of statistical fractals. Similarly, Leonardo da Vinci is renowned for his scientific illustrations of turbulent water dating back to 1500, yet his representations of swirling water fail to capture the statistical fractal quality generated by turbulence. In 1999 I showed that the drip process developed by Jackson Pollock generated statistical fractals similar to those found in Nature's patterns. Pollock's astonishing achievement has been called "fractal expressionism," to distinguish it from the statistical fractals that appeared with the advent of computer art in the 1980s. Pollock's method was not one of "number crunching" and intellectual deliberation but an intuitive process in which the fractal character was established after two minutes of intense activity. Lee Krasner (Pollock's wife and a respected artist) believed that his talent lay in an ability to paint three-dimensional patterns in the air and anticipate how the paint would condense onto the two-dimensional surface of the canvas. Pollock's paintings thus demonstrate that it is possible to create statistical fractals in three-dimensional space. However, to design a building based on statistical fractals, an architect would have to create similar three-dimensional statistical fractals but with the added restriction that the design would have to be assembled into a structurally-sound object.

What are the possible motivations for creating a building based on statistical fractals? Such fractals have a large surface area to volume ratio. For example, trees are built from statistical fractals in order to maximise exposure to the sunlight. Similarly, bronchial trees in our lungs maximise oxygen absorption into the blood vessels. Possible advantages of this large surface area for buildings therefore include solar cells on the rooftops and windows that deliver a large amount of light to the building's interior. However, the main reason for such a design focuses on the associated aesthetics and the hope of mimicking a natural "organic" shape. How would an observer react to an artificial object that assumes a natural fractal form? The study of aesthetic judgement of fractal patterns constitutes a relatively new research field within perception psychology. Only recently have researchers started to quantify people's visual preferences for fractal content. The visual appearance of a statistical fractal object is influenced by a parameter called the fractal dimension D. This quantifies the visual complexity of the fractal pattern. Its value lies between 1 and 2 and moves closer to 2 as the visual complexity increases. This is demonstrated opposite for drip paintings (three images on the left) and corresponding natural scenery (three images on the right). Starting top left, the smooth straight line is visually uncomplicated and has a base D value of 1. An equivalent pattern in nature is the horizon. Moving down, the fractal drip painting is a very sparse, simple pattern with a D value of 1.3. Equivalent fractal patterns in nature are clouds. Moving down, the fractal drips are very rich, intricate and complex with a much higher D value of 1.9. Equivalent fractal patterns in nature are trees in the forest.

Since the D value of a fractal pattern has such a profound impact on its visual appearance, a crucial question is whether people prefer patterns characterised by a particular D value. In 1995, Cliff Pickover used a computer to generate fractal patterns with different D values and found that people expressed a preference for fractal patterns with a high value of 1.8. However, a survey by Deborah Aks and Julien Sprott also used a computer but with a different mathematical method for generating the fractals. This survey reported much lower preferred values of 1.3. The discrepancy between the two surveys would suggest that there is no

Drip paintings   Corresponding natural scenery

universally preferred D value but that the aesthetic qualities of fractals depend specifically on how the fractals are generated. To determine if there are any "universal" aesthetic qualities of fractals, I collaborated with psychologists Branka Spehar, Colin Clifford and Ben Newell. We performed perception studies incorporating the three fundamental categories of fractals: "natural" (scenery such as trees, mountains, clouds, etc.), "mathematical" (computer simulations) and "human" (cropped sections of Pollock's dripped paintings). Participants in the perception study consistently expressed a preference for fractals with D values in the range 1.3 to 1.5, irrespective of the pattern's origin. Significantly, many of the fractal patterns surrounding us in Nature have D values in this mid range.

Recent scientific investigations indicate that the appeal of mid-range fractals extends beyond that of visual aesthetics – these fractals actually reduce the stress of an observer. In a study by James Wise, people were seated facing a 1m by 2m artwork and were asked to perform a sequence of stress-inducing mental tasks such as arithmetic problems, with each task separated by a one-minute recovery period. During this sequence, Wise continuously monitored each person's skin conductance. Skin conductance measurements are a well-established method for quantifying stress – heightened perspiration under stress decreases the skin conductance. The amount of stress induced by mental work can therefore be quantified by the increase in skin conductance DG between the rest and work periods – a large DG value indicates high stress. Wise used the three art works shown above: a realistic photograph of a forest scene, an artistic rendition of a natural landscape, and a pattern of painted lines, together with a uniform white panel serving as a control. DG was found to depend on which artwork was observed. For the "artificial" pattern of lines, DG was 13% greater than for the white control panel indicating that this artwork actually increased the observer's stress. In contrast, the DG values for the "natural" images were 3% (middle) and

44% (left) lower than for the control, indicating a reduction in stress. This result confirms an earlier proposal that natural images might be incorporated into artificial environments as a method of stress reduction. Why, though, was the middle image far more effective in reducing stress than the left image? To answer this question I recently teamed up with Wise and performed a fractal analysis of the two images. Significantly, the D value of the middle natural image was found to be 1.4, lying within the category of fractals previously established as being visually appealing. In contrast, the image on the left had a D value of 1.6, lying outside the visually pleasing range. It appears then that the appeal of mid-range fractal patterns (D=1.3 to 1.5) extends beyond simple visual aesthetics and is sufficient to deliver a profound physiological impact on the observer.

This is potentially exciting news for Frank Gehry and his "cloud-like" design: clouds are fractal patterns with a D value of 1.3 that lies within the "magic" range of preferred visual complexity. But will the design be capable of mimicking the fractal character of Nature's clouds? The challenge may not be as difficult as it seems. Contrary to popular belief, Nature's fractals do not repeat over many magnifications. Whereas computer-generated fractals repeat from finitely large to infinitesimally small magnifications, typical fractals only repeat over a magnification range of twenty-five. Thus, for a cloud-like building, the largest features would only have to be a factor of twenty-five bigger than the smallest features. This is challenging but not impossible. Furthermore, the low D value of a cloud ensures that the fractal structure will be relatively smooth and sparse. If Gehry had chosen a forest-like fractal structure, the intricacy and complexity of this high D fractal structure would have been much more difficult to incorporate into a building.

If this proposal does become reality, it will be fascinating to see if people's fundamental appreciation of fractal clouds will inspire New Yorkers to embrace Frank Gehry's revolutionary building design.

above: a realistic rendition of a natural landscape; *middle* : an artistic rendition of a natural landscape; *right* : a pattern of painted lines

RICHARD TAYLOR

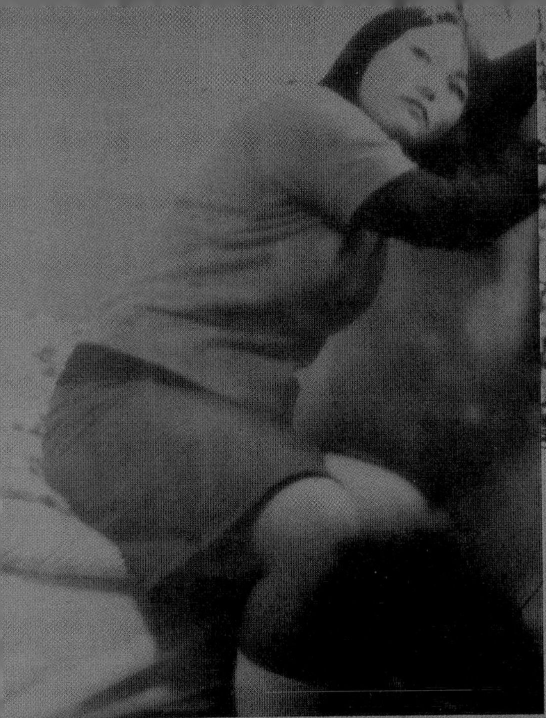
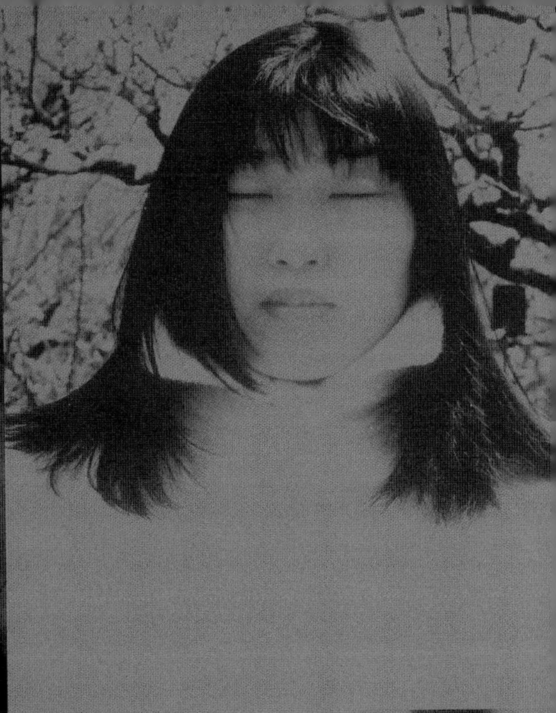
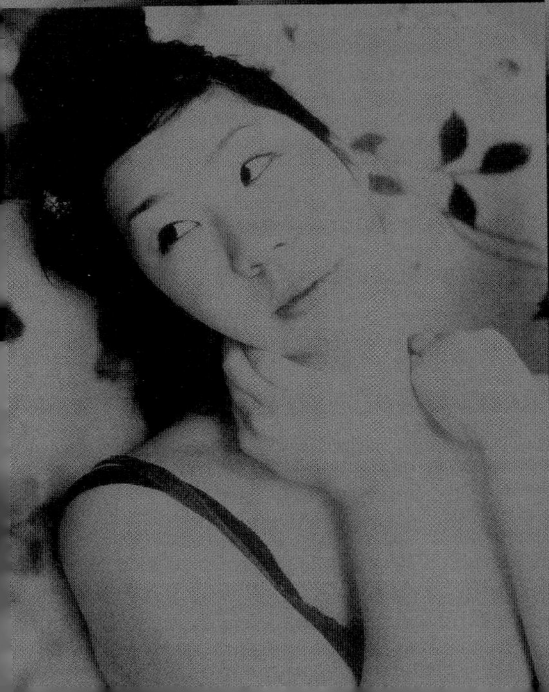
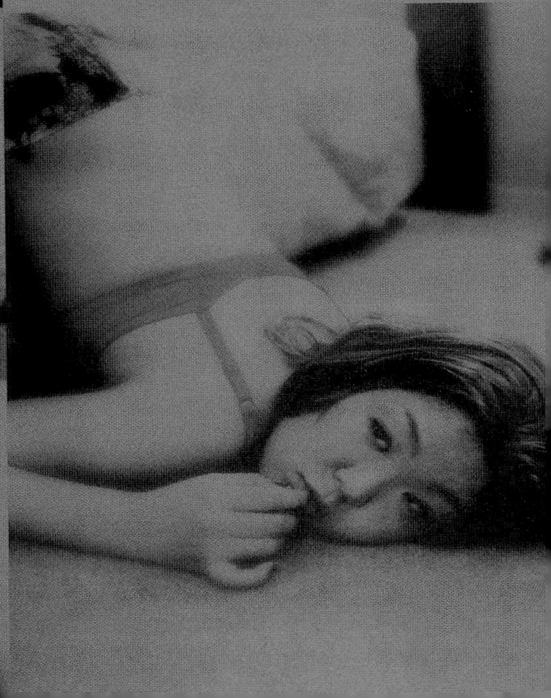

◀ Portrait photograph of present-day girls in Japan. Photos: Hallen van Meene.

ARATA ISOZAKI

City of Girls
Tokyo – An Alien Metropolis

Like life within an environment constantly under phosphorescent lighting, everything looks flat and indistinguishable and this creature Girl has no knowledge of how to deal with the dark

New Architecture 7: *Innovation – From Experimentation to Realisation*, 2003

Kosuke Tsumura – *Final Home* ▶

Let me first define the meaning of Girls as "that splendid existence" which occurs before a young female is drawn into a system of gender-bias, and the separation of masculinity and femininity. The poet, William Wordsworth, once said of youth: "… Nothing can bring back the hour / Of splendour in the grass, of glory in the flower." Yet, Girls today are *déracinées* – a French word meaning rootless weeds. In the Japanese family system, the framework of a father-dominated structure disappeared long ago. Today's Girls find that the only secure proof of their existence is in their bodies… they flow and roam in and around the city. There is no conscious decision forming a division between what is inside and what is outside. Like life within an environment constantly under phosphorescent lighting, everything looks flat and indistinguishable and this creature Girl has no knowledge of how to deal with the dark. But she is not isolated: her thumb is in constant movement – in communication on a cellular phone with her friends.

Throughout history she has pursued the ideal of Pure Beauty. When she judges adults as ugly, she has an immediate physical response towards the object of disgust. The materialistic, media-oriented environments of the multi-layered city amplify her metaphysical reactions to that physical stimulus.

The entire psychological and even the physical existence of these Girls has become a sensory apparatus. And these sensors are at the core of the contemporary city. The way these Girls live may strike us as negative because of their combination of toughness and taste for kitsch but I would like to discover in them the future of the 21st century City.

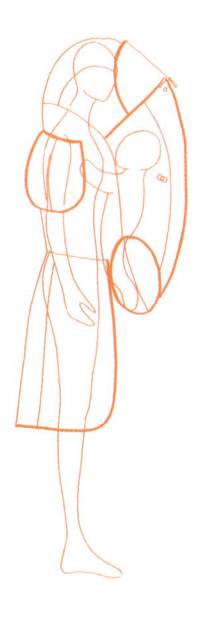

Looking back to that point when Girls' comics were born in the 1970s, we should probably have predicted the appearance of the kind of Girls we now see, who have such a tremendous impact on the cities of Japan. Amazingly, the faces and body language of the Girls appearing in the illustrated media at that time were largely dismissed as cheap stereotypes, while they were already evolving into new standards of social communication for Girls and Girls-to-be. Totally different from the female image of any previous age, this new Girl was developing into a printed heroine while also generating the impetus for the red carpet introduction of her virtual reality counterparts in the age of digital media.

It is remarkable that the character of the real Girls developed out of this artificial imagery and that Girls of matching body proportions derived from cartoon prototypes began filling the streets of Japanese cities with figures exhibiting nearly identical skin colour, eyes, voices, faces and make-up.

In Japanese, the word *kawaii* is one that fits all circumstances and expresses the perceived charming qualities of dress, accessories, interior design and…well, everything. Literally meaning "cute," the word is most often used to indicate a trendy fetishism that implies a depth of caring – even love – for a material thing or media object.

When the majority of Girls show an interest in an item or product, it quickly emerges as a mainstream trend in the consumer marketplace. "Loose socks" (thick cotton long socks which are worn loosely hanging between the knee and ankle), *Tamagotchi* (the digital pet which must be fed and nurtured to prevent it from dying), and the newest *Keitai* (cellular phones) are just a few of the many products that have been vitalised in the Japanese market by these Girls. It is not a question of taste: once something has been declared THEIR favourite, THEIR territory, its status as such is all that matters.

The city in such cases may not be too far removed from the urban images in the film *Blade Runner* where Rachael represents the artificially idealised, stylised android woman – manmade and provided with implanted memories of a non-existent childhood, as well as computer created snapshots of herself at six with parents she never really had, supporting and renewing the manufactured memories.

In the same way, each of us has private memories to help us establish our identities and grasp the reality of our own existence. Take these memories away and what is left? And what about the Girls of the new millennium…especially those who do not have fond memories of a real home and a vital urban existence? The single-minded determination when they choose even a trivial course of action may be the result of desperation and an insecurity that adults can never really fully fathom.

Girls say that they have to generate their own memories and establish memories of the present and of the future. The blank spaces created by the architects Sejima/Nishizawa provide a floating space in time where these Girls can begin to wander among their new reminiscences. Do they dream of sheep I wonder?*

The term *Shōjo Toshi* (City of Girls) first appeared in the title of a *Jōkyo Gekijyou* (Red Tent Theatre Troupe) play by Jyuro Kara in 1969.

Do Androids Dream of Electric Sheep? is a 1968 Sci-Fi novel by Philip K. Dick that provided source material for *Blade Runner*

Portrait photograph of present-day girls in Japan. Photos: Hallen van Meene. ▶

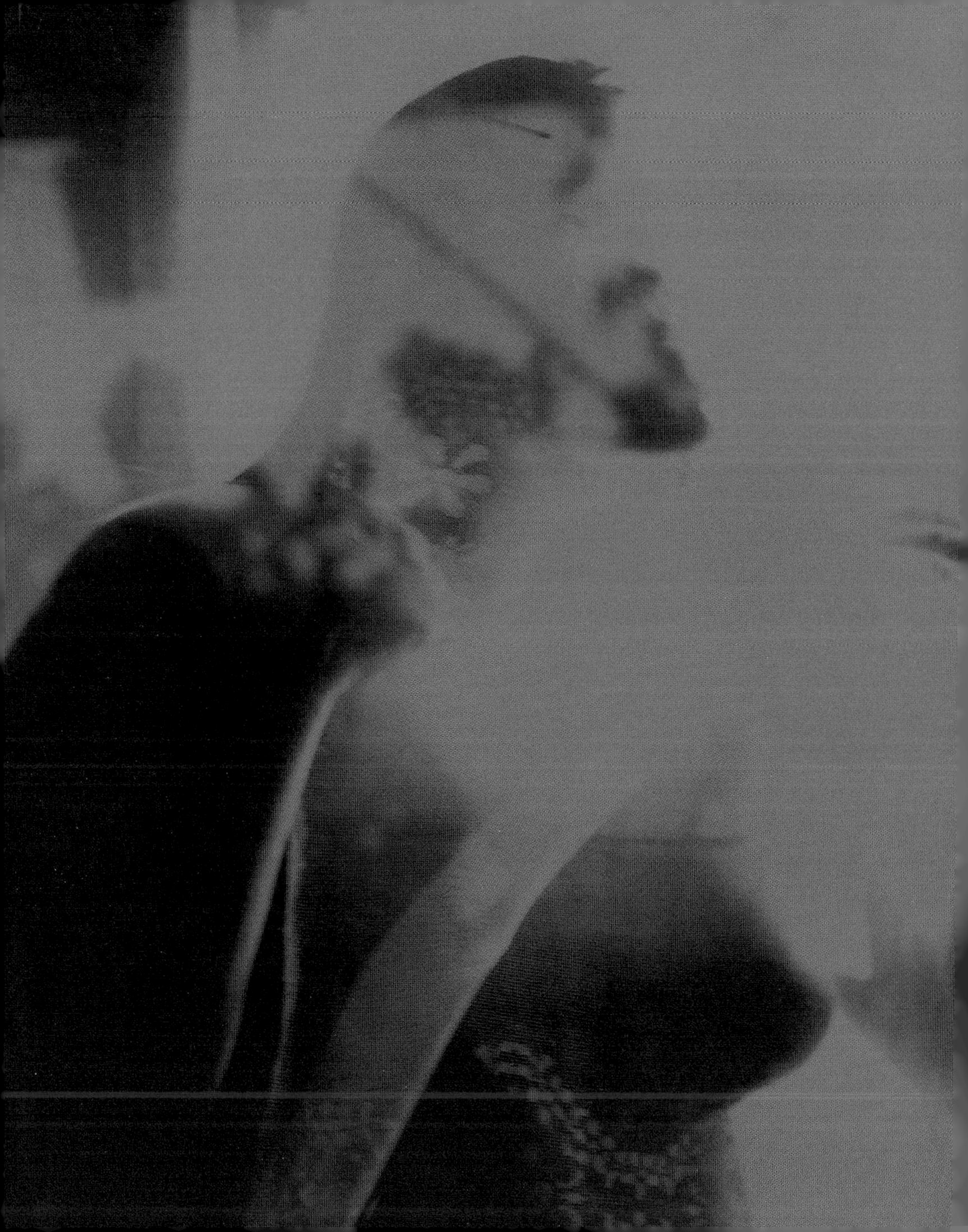

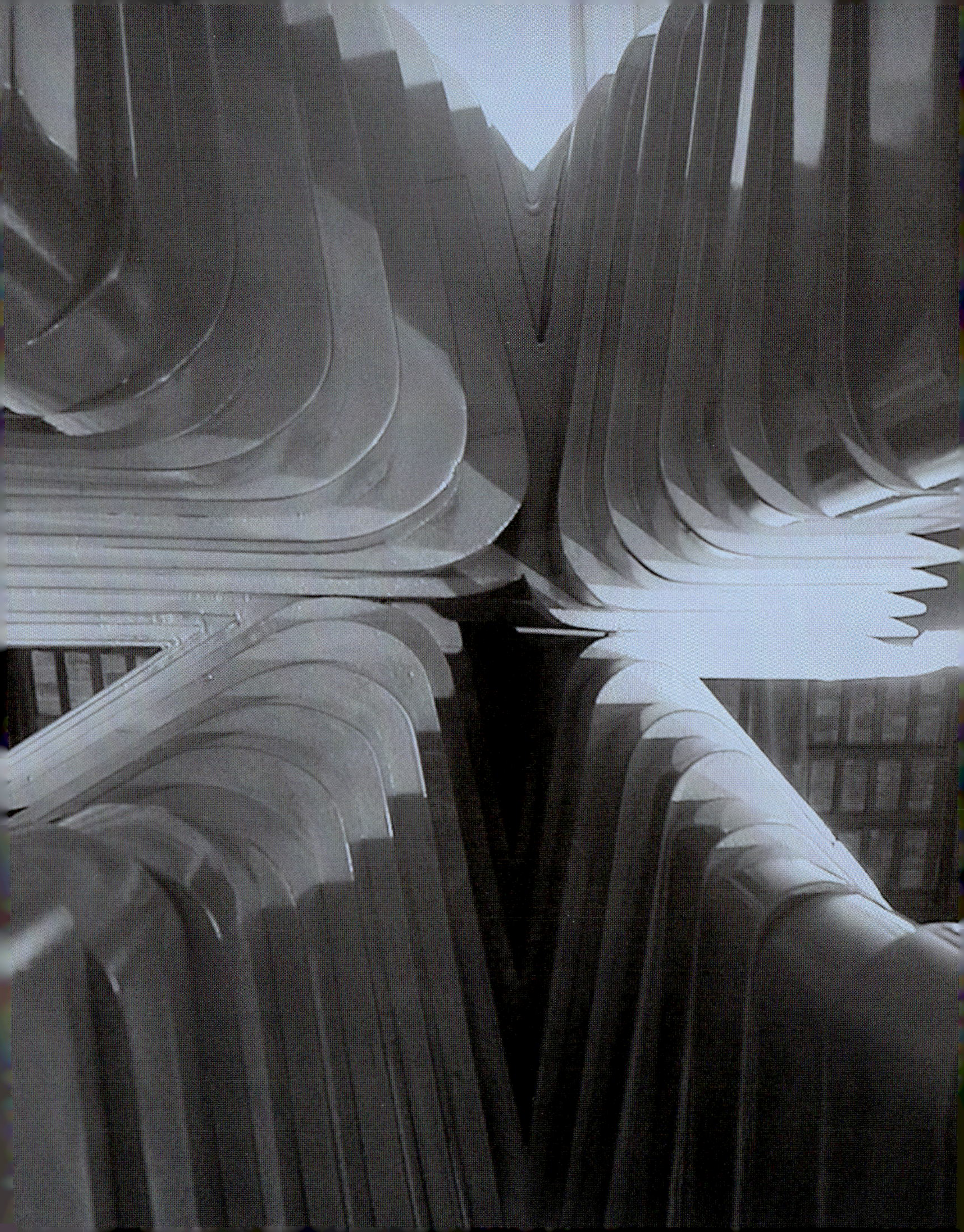

◄ Zaha Hadid Architects, World Trade Center; installation at Venice Biennale 2002

PATRIK SCHUMACHER

What's Next?
From Destructive Impact
to Creative Impulse

*Zaha Hadid Architects believes that large components
of the contemporary metropolis must be conceived as
evolving rather than finished, fixed structures*

The tragic destruction of the World Trade Center raises the question of what could replace it. Rather than calling for a symbolic response the question is what kind of organisational structure would satisfy contemporary business life and what kind of formal language would articulate it? What are the functionality and aesthetics of the contemporary metropolis? How – if at all – should its essence appear on the Manhattan Skyline?

New York's World Trade Center was one of the largest and most ambitious structures ever built.

This complex – comprising the twin towers plus five lower buildings – was designed by Minoru Yamasaki in the mid-to-late 1960s. This was at the peak of the era of Fordism – the system of assembly-line mass production that led to modern mass society organised around huge corporations. The World Trade Center was one of the culminating investments of the long post-war boom. Construction of the towers started in 1969 and was completed in 1973. The Twin Towers alone offered one million square metres of office space spread over 110 storeys. The total centre offered working space for fifty thousand people. This is equivalent to the population of a medium-sized city.

Fordism in general was marked by massive endeavours. Everything was produced in bulk and everything was based on standardisation and reproduction. Grids, series, and the repetition of the same! The serial aesthetic of Mies van der

Zaha has one of the clearest architectural trajectories we've seen in many years. Each project unfolds with new excitement and innovation

Frank Gehry

Rohe's American period was the most pertinent expression of Fordism in architecture. Yamasaki's twin towers developed this principle to its ultimate symbolic conclusion: even such an enormous, iconic structure as the great American skyscraper could be subordinated to the principle of repetition.

The repetition of the same operates between the two towers as well as within each individual tower.

The epoch of the skyscraper is over, not primarily for security concerns but because the organizational structure of the skyscraper is too simple and too constricting. Towers grow in only one dimension. The strict linearity of their extension accounts for their characteristic poverty of connectivity. Towers are hermetic units, which are themselves arrays of equally hermetic units (floors). These features of linearity and strict segmentation are antithetical to contemporary business relations as well as to contemporary urban life in general. Much higher levels of complexity are required to spatially order and articulate contemporary relations.

ARCHITECTURE AS URBANISM

The demise of Fordism and of the skyscraper as its urban archetype does not imply the retreat from the large scale nor from high density. Both size and density are increasing within the contemporary metropolis.

The exhaustion of historic city centres – there are simply not enough of them to satisfy the insatiable need for contemporary urbanity – and the bankruptcy of comprehensive city planning in the face of market uncertainty, means that architecture has to carry the burden of urbanism within large single developments. Architecture has been mostly overburdened by this task. However, new spatial models should be able to organise higher levels of complexity and integrate significantly more simultaneous programmatic agendas and divers life-processes.

But how can appropriate spatial patterns be invented and how can the required spatial complexity be built up? The task is to devise strategies to produce large buildings that fulfil the function of urban communication and exchange.

Zaha Hadid Architects would project an entity of a higher order than what is usually deemed to be a "building" or even an "ensemble," an entity that recreates within itself approximations of the multiplicity, complexity and effectiveness of the urban: a city compressed into a large building.

In addition, the time factor should be introduced in scenarios of phasing and reconfiguration. Zaha Hadid Architects believes that large components of the contemporary metropolis must be conceived as evolving rather than finished, fixed structures.

This significant site should be tackled only after sufficient intellectual and creative resources have been gathered, i.e. after the architects are satisfied that their intervention has a chance of articulating the essential operations and ambitions of the contemporary metropolis with the same poignancy and profundity that made the World Trade Center such an effective symbol of modern civilisation.

Approaching the task in this spirit opens up the opportunity to realise a large-scale urban intervention with a significant transformative impulse for the whole of Manhattan.

Installation at Venice Biennale 2002 ▶

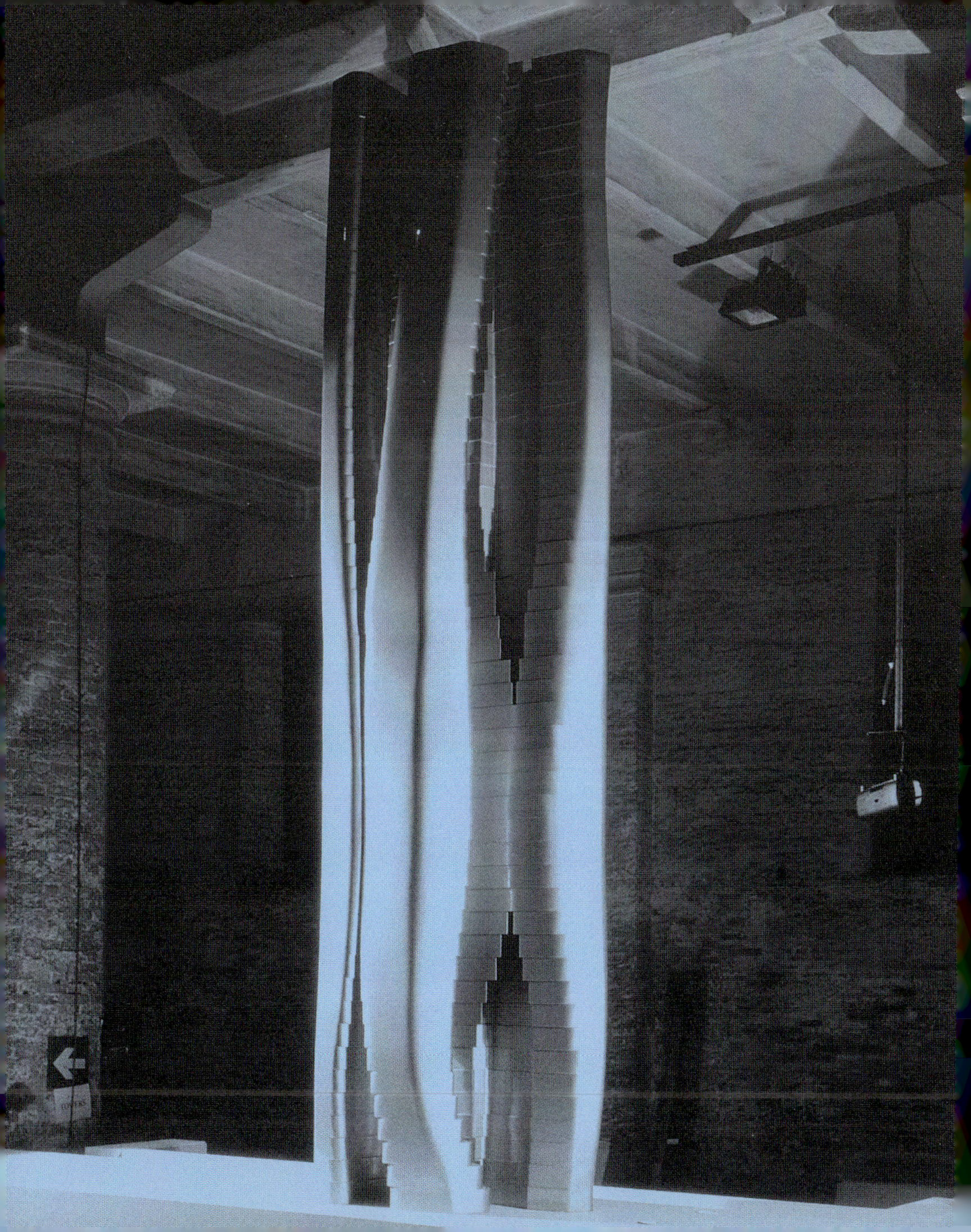

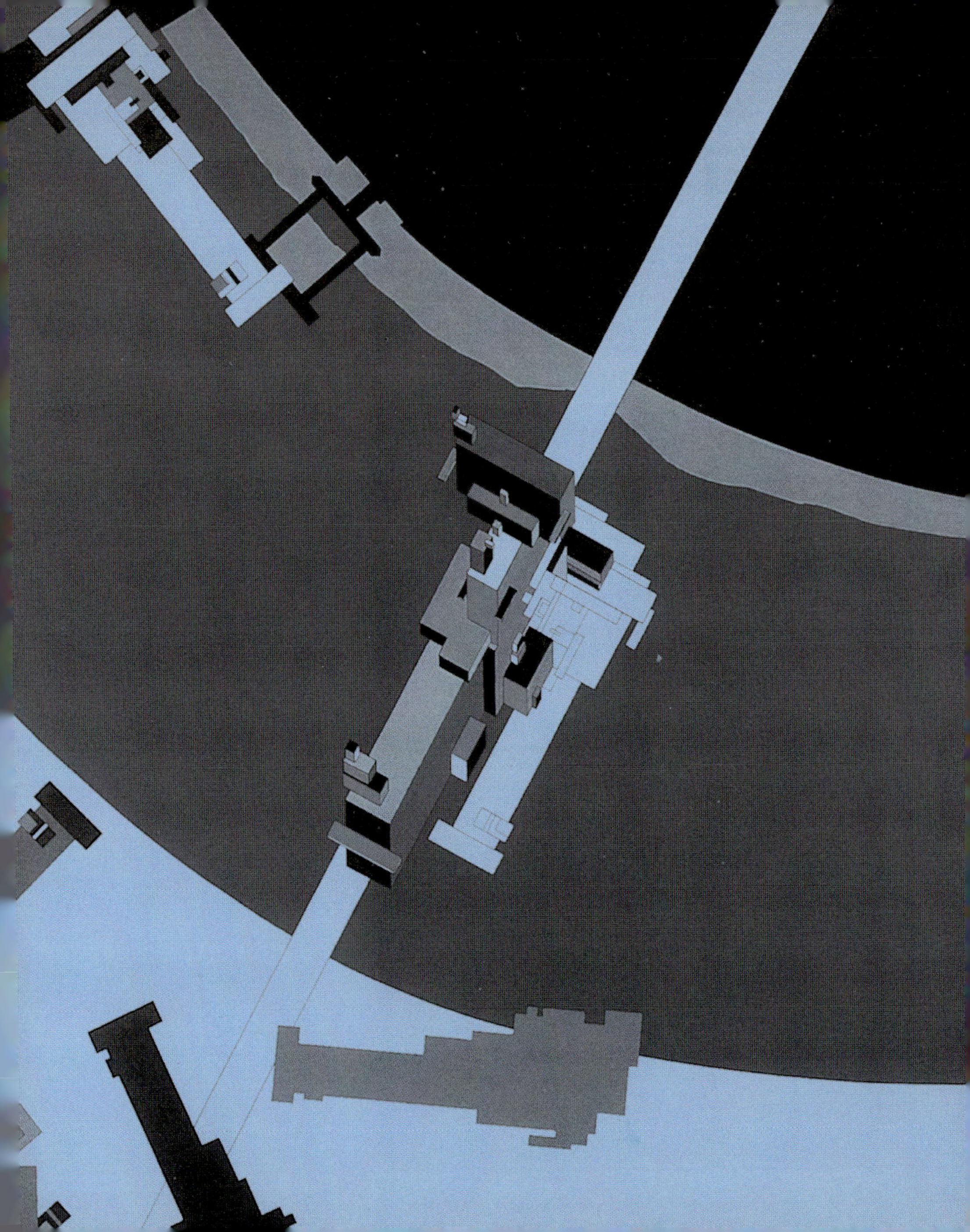

◀ *Malevich's Tektonik* Zaha Hadid, 1976-1977

PATRIK SCHUMACHER

Aspects of the Work of Zaha Hadid

In the early 1980s Zaha Hadid burst onto the architectural scene with a series of spectacular designs embodied by even more spectacular drawings and paintings

One of the most significant and momentous features of the architectural avant-garde of the last twenty years is the proliferation of representational media and design processes. In the early 1980s Zaha Hadid burst onto the architectural scene with a series of spectacular designs embodied by even more spectacular drawings and paintings. The idiosyncrasies of these drawings made it difficult to read them as straightforward architectural descriptions. This initial openness of interpretation might have led some commentators to suspect 'mere graphics' here.

But this predicament to start (and ultimately stay) with two-dimensional drawings has been architecture's predicament ever since its inception as a discipline distinguished from construction. As Robin Evans pointed out so bluntly: architects do not build, they draw.

Therefore the translation from drawing to building might be problematic – at least under conditions of innovation. Architecture as a design discipline that is distinguished from the physical act of building constitutes itself on the basis of drawing. The discipline of architecture emerges and separates from the craft of construction through the systematic

> The predicament to start with two-dimensional drawings has been architecture's predicament ever since its inception as a discipline distinguished from construction. As Robin Evans pointed out so bluntly: architects do not build, they draw

differentiation of the drawing as tool and domain of expertise outside (and in advance) of the material process of construction. The first effect of drawing (in ancient Greek architecture) seems to be an increased capacity for standardization, precision and regularized reproduction on a fairly high level of complexity and across a rather wide territory. Roman architecture could benefit from this but also hints at the exploitation of the capacity of invention that the medium of drawing affords. Without drawing the typological proliferation of Roman architecture is inconceivable. Since the Renaissance (via Mannerism and the Baroque) this speculative moment of drawing has been gathering momentum. But only 1920s' modernism really discovered the full power and potential of drawing as a highly economic trial-error mechanism and an effortless plane of invention.

In this respect, modern architecture depends upon the revolution within the visual arts that finally shook off the burden of representation. Modern architecture was able to build upon the legacy of modern abstract art as the conquest of a previously unimaginable realm of constructive freedom. Hitherto, art was understood as mimesis and the reiteration of given subjects, i.e. representation rather than creation. Architecture was the representation of a fixed set of minutely determined typologies and complete tectonic systems. Against this backdrop abstraction meant the possibility and challenge of free creation. The canvas became the field of an original construction. A monumental breakthrough with enormous consequences for the whole of modern civilisation. Through figures such as Malevich and vanguard groups such as the de Stijl movement this exhilarating historical moment was captured and exploited for the world of experimental architecture.

The thesis here is that the withdrawal into the two-dimensional surface, i.e. the refusal to interpret everything immediately as a spatial representation, is a condition for the full exploitation of the medium of drawing as a medium of invention. Only on this basis, as explicitly graphic manoeuvres, do the design manoeuvres gain enough fluidity and freedom to come into play. They have to be set free to shake off the burden of always already meaning something specific.

Such a stage of play and proliferation must, of course, be followed by concentrated work on selection and interpretation. At some stage architectural work leads to building. But not in every project. Some architectural projects remain on paper to be 'translated' later into other projects. The discipline of architecture has learned to allow for this and many great contributions to architectural history have been made in this way.

One of Hadid's audacious moves was to translate the dynamism and fluidity of her calligraphic hand directly into equally fluid tectonic systems. Another was the move from isometric and perspective projection to literal distortions of space and from exploded axonometry to the literal explosion of space into fragments, from the superimposition of various fish-eye perspectives to the literal bending and meltdown of space. Such moves initially appeared illogical, akin to the operations of the Surrealists.

The apparently mindless sketching and endless variation on graphic textures operates like an 'abstract machine' proliferating difference in order to make a selection.

Once a strange texture or figure is selected and confronted with a programmatic agenda a peculiar form-content dialectic is engendered. An active figure-reading mind will find the desired conditions. In addition, new desires and functions are inspired by the encounter with the strange configuration. The radically irrational and arbitrary detour finds its way to the target.

This 'miracle' can be explained by a recognition that all functionality is relative, that all well-articulated organisms were once monstrous aberrations and may later seem to be crude and deficient in relation to other 'higher' and more 'beautiful' organisms. Before we dismiss arbitrary formalisms we need to realise that all our time-tested typologies adhere dogmatically to the arbitrary formalism of orthogonality and Platonic simplicity, derived from the constraints of measuring, making and stabilising structures handed down to us from a relatively primitive stage of our civilisation. To remain locked within these figures in this age would be more than arbitrary. Our only way out is radical proliferation and testing of other options. All points of departure are equally arbitrary until tested against presumed criteria. There is no absolute. Every measure starts with a finite array of arbitrary options to compare, select from and adapt, thus working away from absolute arbitrariness. It is significant that the logic of evolutionary innovation starts with mutation: mutation, selection and reproduction. Hadid has been a vital engine of mutation with respect to architectural culture.

The level of experimentation reached a point where the distinction between form and content within these drawings and paintings, was no longer fixed. The question as to which features of the graphic manipulation pertain to the mode of representation rather than to the object of representation has been left unanswered. Was the architecture itself twisting, bending, fragmenting and interpenetrating? Or were these features just aspects of the multi-view-point fish-eye perspectives? In fact, over the course of an extended process and a long chain of projects the graphic features have slowly transfigured into spatial features that could be put into effect. The initial openness may have led some commentators to suspect 'mere graphics', but within Zaha Hadid's studio that openness was productively engaged, through a slow process of interpretation, via further drawings, projects and – finally – buildings.

Once seriously applied within the context of an architectural project, these strange moves – which seemed so alien and crazy – turned out to be powerful compositional options capable of articulating complex programmes. The dynamic streams of movements within a complex structure can now be made legible; they are clearly the most fluid regions within the structure; overall trapezoidal distortions offer one more way to respond to non-orthogonal sites;

perspective distortions allow the orientation of elements to various functional focal points. What was once an outrageous violation of logic has become part of a strategically deployed repertoire of nuanced spatial organisation and articulation.

Painterly techniques like colour modulations, gradients of dark to light, pointillist techniques and dissolving objects in their background, all assume significance in terms of the articulation of new design concepts such as morphing, or new spatial concepts such as smooth thresholds, 'field-space', and the 'space of becoming' (Eisenman). Jeff Kipnis deserves recognition as someone who has theorised the possibilities of 'graphic space'. But it was Zaha Hadid who went first and furthest in exploring this method of introducing innovation in architecture.

Hadid used axonometric and perspective projection in a new way to give dynamism to the implied space. Such projections were deployed at first according to their proper function as a means of representation. It soon became apparent, however, that there was a 'self-serving' fascination with the sort of extreme distortion of spaces and objects that emerged from the ruthless application of perspective construction – not like the anamorphic projections one can find in certain seventeenth-century paintings. Hadid built up pictorial spaces within which multiple perspective constructions were fused into a seamless dynamic texture. One way to understand these images is to see them as attempts to emulate the experience of moving through an architectural composition revealing a succession of rather different points of view. Another, more radical way of reading them is to divorce oneself from the implied views and to read the swarms of distorted forms as a peculiar architectural world in its own right, a world with its own characteristic forms, compositional laws and spatial effects.

One of the most striking features of these large canvases is the strong sense of coherence despite the richness and diversity of forms they contain. There is never monotonous repetition, the field continuously changing its scalar grain. Gradient transitions mediate large quiet areas with very dense and intense zones. These compositions are usually polycentral and multidirectional. All these features are the result of using multiple, interpenetrating perspective projections. Often the dynamic intensity of the overall field is increased by using curved instead of straight projection lines. Such projective geometry allows an arbitrarily large and diverse set of elements to be brought within its unifying law of diminution and distortion. The resultant graphic space anticipates the later (and still very much current) concepts of field and swarm. The effect achieved is very similar to those effects currently being pursued with curvilinear mesh-deformations and digitally simulated 'gravitational fields' that grip, align, orient and thus cohere a set of elements or particles within the digital model.

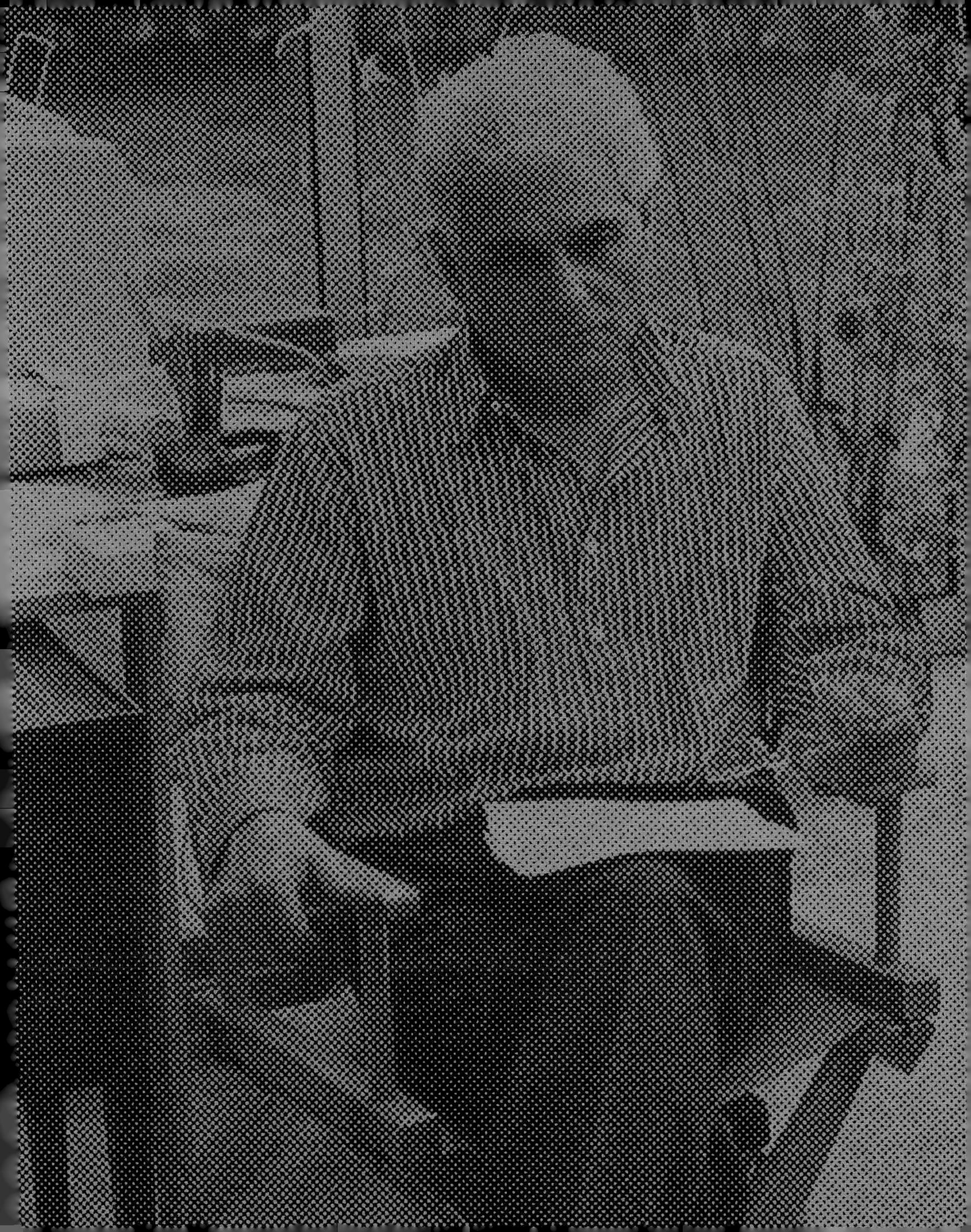

◀ Jacques Derrida at home in his studio being interviewed for *Architectural Design*

ANDREAS PAPADAKIS

Philosophy and Architecture
A partnership for the future?

From ancient times, architecture, considered an imitative art like painting and sculpture, was denied a Muse, since it required no guidance other than from nature

Paper Art 6: Deconstructivist Tendencies, Cantz Verlag, 1996

Over the last decade a curious situation has been developing in architecture, a kind of shotgun wedding with philosophy aiming to enable architecture to respond to a fast-changing world and a nebulous future. The roles of the architect and the philosopher are becoming more and more intertwined. Derrida himself is surprised at the ready response of architects to his work.

In his public address to architects – in the event on video – he explains: "…When I first met, I won't say 'Deconstructive architecture', but the Deconstructive discourse on architecture, I was rather puzzled and suspicious. I thought at first perhaps this was an analogy, a displaced discourse, and something more analogical than rigorous. And then I realised that on the contrary, the most efficient way of putting Deconstruction to work was by going through art and architecture."

The story of how Peter Eisenman came to collaborate with Jacques Derrida on Bernard Tschumi's Parc de la Villette is familiar. Less well-known within architectural circles, but deeply influential, is the work of Gilles Deleuze, who has produced a sustained body of dense conceptual work on the fold. Deleuze's analysis of the fold makes direct links between philosophy and architecture, that have not been overlooked by architects, led by Eisenman, who has actually applied Deleuze's folding theory to the design of buildings.

Eisenman is not alone in his appreciation of complex philosophical and mathematical theory to construction projects. Over the past two decades a curious situation has developed in architecture whereby it has practically divided itself into two separate disciplines, one intellectually charged, with its main field of activity teaching in the new universities, and the other section practical, operating on building sites controlled increasingly by commercial interests. To the outsider at least, the goals of the first camp appear to be the construction of a complex theory, guaranteed to exclude all but those in the know; while those of the second appear to be compelled but greed. The two seemed to be mutually exclusive. The practitioners of the second category had simply given up any attempt to put intellectual life into their productions, while the academics of the first often claimed that to build their paper projects would be to contaminate the purity of their conception.

However, in recent years a change has taken place in the attitude of the theoreticians who have become building architects while remaining university professors.

It is in this environment that the architect as teacher is taking a more significant role. One of the reasons that the introduction of Deconstruction to architectural thinking is considered significant is that with few exceptions architecture has consistently lacked contact with other disciplines like philosophy. From ancient times architecture, considered an imitative art like painting and sculpture, was denied a Muse since it required no guidance other than from nature. This attitude was reinforced by the founders of the medieval universities who denied it a faulty, relegating teaching to schools with the emphasis on design and technology – a practice continuing well into the twentieth century.

Today's intellectual avant-garde in architecture has been spear-headed from America, where a society with profoundly mixed cultural roots has produced trained architects, who established a reputation through their writings, university research and paper projects, long before being invited to build anything. But just when academic events are proliferating all over the world, the original theorists have moved to that other world of architectural construction, taking on some of the largest and most prestigious projects of recent years.

Their buildings met with most mixed response and were both criticised and praised. Despite the scepticism of the committed anti-theoretical lobby, who argue that architecture should spring from the hands rather than from the head, their qualities are compelling.

Amongst the generation of architects nurtured in the heady atmosphere of theoretical debate which has thrived during the last decade, Bernard Tschumi and Daniel Libeskind in particular have made their mark. Both born and educated in Europe, they gravitated to the States early in their careers. Tschumi's appointment as Dean of Architecture at Columbia University seemed like a final symbolic mark of acceptance into the academic architectural establishment; but, simultaneously, his architectural practice started to expand. It began with the assignment to design and construct the Parc de la Villette and its folies in Paris in 1983; now he is busy working on several major new projects including a building for Columbia University and an institute of architecture in Paris.

Likewise, Libeskind, the paper architect par excellence, who delights in an obscure prose/poetry style in his writings (his dissertation at the University of Essex was on Imagination and Space), is going through a similar development. His Jewish Museum in Berlin nears completion and he has just signed a contract for a new extension to London's Victoria and Albert Museum. Libeskind, too, has become a practising architect.

For over a decade now media coverage of the new architectural language has been enormous. According to Tschumi, one consequence of the shift of attention towards the surface has been the majority of objects of architectural history can be seen merely as sketches or drawings, not as actual buildings. By far the most important influence on recent architecture has been the magazines that publish paper architecture. But now the dreamers of the past decades are building for real.

This move of the theoretical architects into construction, at a time of enormous public ignorance and Philistinism in architecture is a surprising phenomenon and a great achievement; it also marks a major change of attitude on the part of the architects themselves, who have not in the past placed much emphasis on the need to build. The critics have had to take theory on board in their assessment of a building, rather than reducing their elucidation to an exercise in pure structural logic and material forces. The theoretical architect aspire to transcend the preoccupations of Modernism by establishing a contemporary architecture suited to our uncertain and swiftly changing times. The unfamiliar and often unsettling forms which they use emerge not out of constructional, but out of philosophical considerations, translated into three-dimensionality by means of complex mathematical calculation

The controversial French mathematician, René Thom with his work on catastrophe theory, with its inevitable connotations of Doomsday, has provided a convenient starting point for a number of architects, including Bahram Shirdel who has actually used mathematical equations to create three-dimensional volumes. Hani Rashid and Lise Anne Couture of Asymptote Architecture present perhaps the most direct architectural response in their Light Prop experimental studies of fringes and other uncharted zones: "From a single catastrophic moment a space emerges made only of light. The space undergoes unforeseen changes and is without form or structure. Then, in an instant, a vast array of elements is revealed, each one folding upon the other, reconfiguring limitless possibilities. We are now at the threshold an uncharted landscape, well beyond the sanctuary of order and reason. Here concealed beyond places inviting yearning and anticipation, we discover an architecture that perseveres."

They are, of course, responding to René Thom's mathematical solutions which concentrate on sudden discontinuities – catastrophes – where he defines the role of theoretician who observes the continuous creation and destruction of forms, foresees changes and, where possible, explains them.

The idea of fragmentation and deconstruction in society and culture is at the core of the work of most theoretical architects. Peter Eisenman describes it as 'mediated culture': a condition in which everything we know is mediated through images with which we are bombarded every day continuously increases. The result is that the image takes on a reality and validity of its own – illusion become interchangeable with reality. The systems by which we have understood the world in the past break down because our preconceptions are under constant bombardment. Time and space themselves have been manipulated and no longer have constant, dependable value. Nothing can remain still and static anymore, and traditional values, formulated by different societies inhabiting a quite different world, have, as a result, lost their relevance.

Tschumi expresses these concepts with a lucidity rare in this field of architectural discourse. He has stated quite clearly the impossibility of returning to the 'comforting fiction' of the eighteenth-century village'. Set up by architectural revivalists and conservationists as the answer to the confusions and conflicts experienced by society in the modern world which they have created but cannot come to terms with. Here, no concession to pluralism is made!

Eisenman's work, which is the very essence of abstraction and elitism, is a reaction against Modernism's preoccupation with function, and the conception of design as the product of some oversimplified form-follows-function formula. This has led him to a type of formalism where the programme and its significance are diminished in order to draw attention to the form.

The isolation of pure design in the work of architectural theorists, and their move into construction. Has angered many critics and commentators. The vision of Modernists was narrowly focussed on a new Utopia in which mass production would radically improve the standard of living for the masses. But such dogmatism was not really an answer to the incredible uncertainty that mass alienation, dispossession, suffering, and a collapse of values caused by the world was has created.

Contemporary theorists and practitioners have taken this on board and argue that we must embrace the modern condition, and revise our perception of architecture accordingly.

Tschumi's and Eisenman's concept of the architecture of the event represents this complete revision of ideas. Tschumi reinterprets the link between form and function as a non-casual interaction primarily concerned with shock effect. He looks to film as a more appropriate model for producing architecture than aesthetics and structures. In the Manhattan Transcripts, arguably the earliest study on Deconstruction, he produced what he called frame-by-frame descriptions of an architectural inquest...They propose to transcribe an architectural interpretation of reality...plans, section, and diagrams outline spaces and indicate the movements of the different protagonists – those people intruding into the architectural stage set.

In a similar vein, Eisenman has described the rock concert as possibly the only form of architectural event, as a new type of mediated environment which incorporates the audience Itself. He says: 'this kind of event structure is not architecture standing against media, but architecture being consumed by it'.

Tschumi's folies at the Parc de la Villette were perhaps the first concrete manifestation on a significant scale, in an urban public place, of the theories which he had been formulating. Each "folie" was meant to represent a location for an 'event', what he calls a 'turning point', rather than to stand as a traditionally-designed piece of architecture. The result – a series of decorative red structures in the park with no apparent function – is interesting, but not, in fact particularly easy to interpret as a branch of architectural theory. The architect explains:

"Architecture is not an illustrative art; it does not illustrate theories …You cannot design a new definition of the city and its architecture. But you may be able to design the conditions that will make it possible for this non-hierarchical, non-traditional society to happen…"

If Tschumi's buildings are not immediately readable as theoretical statements, it is nonetheless true that they have been generated by a philosophy and a view of life which the author sets much store on promulgating. In this sense, the work must still be regarded as didactic, as must that of the architect – theorists such as Eisenman and Libeskind. The Wexner centre, with its huge superficial grid structure, or the Jewish Museum with its extraordinary, aggressive form and the void inside, are not meant to go unnoticed.

The buildings of the theoretical architects have in common that they are meant to be provocative, to ask questions, to disconcert. Once the theory is behind them, and the process by which it generates the design decisions is understood, each building becomes an impressive intellectual feat and built manifesto. And they are the progeny of the marriage of architecture and philosophy.

"What is Philosophy?" asks Deleuze in one of his last books to be published before his untimely suicide, to which he replies "It is an activity that creates concepts." For Deleuze a concept is signed like a painting. And so, for him, it is a work of art that has to be worked on, polished, turned into a beautiful object, not so that it can be passively admired but so that it can be offered as a tool to those who wish or are able to use it.

This paper is a reworked version of one presented at the Hydra Conference, 1995, and is partly based on the introduction to *Theory and Experimentation*, Academy Editions, London, 1993

Bernard Tschumi – Parc de la Villette, Paris – Superimposition ▶